Body Theology

By the same author:

ARTHUR A. VOGEL

Body Theology

GOD'S PRESENCE IN MAN'S WORLD

HARPER & ROW, PUBLISHERS

NEW YORK, EVANSTON, SAN FRANCISCO, LONDON

ACKNOWLEDGMENTS

All biblical quotations are from the Revised Standard Version of the Bible unless otherwise noted.

FIRST EDITION

STANDARD BOOK NUMBER: 06–068881–5

LIBRARY OF CONGRESS CATALOG CARD NUMBER: 72–11365

88530

To my friends,
both colleagues and students,
at Nashotah House

Contents

Preface

It might seem odd to call a book about personal presence and about God's absolute difference from us as a Person, *Body Theology*. But there are several reasons for the choice of that title. First of all, the emphasis throughout this volume is experiential, and our bodies locate and center our experience in the world. Second, this book—although not lengthy —in many ways summarizes, as well as extends, the theological use I have made over the last decade and a half of secular insights into the nature of man's "lived body."

We know the *personal* presence of other people only as that presence transcends physical objects; in order to specify the nature of personal presence we must contrast it to mere bodily presence. Contrast aside, body relations or the extension of those relations in language are the only means by which we can begin to know persons in the world. The Christian God who wanted human beings to know him as a person became incarnate—took a body—for that very reason.

The recognition of personal presence begins with bodies,

and personal presence, once recognized as the source of radical newness in our lives, makes a difference in the way we live our bodies. Personal presence thus relates immediately to the body in both the beginning and the end. That being the case, any truly "religious theology" of a personal God—any knowledge of God which attempts to be experiential and make a difference in our daily living—must be a "body theology." This claim, of course, can be judged by each reader for himself.

Besides the evolution of this modest volume through my own experience—conditioned by friends, teaching, and selected conferences and lectures—I especially want to thank the Rev. Kenneth R. Clark and Dom Leo Patterson for helpful suggestions on chapters 1 and 3 respectively.

ARTHUR A. VOGEL

The will is under the judgement of God when its fear of death is inverted into fear of committing murder.

—EMMANUEL LEVINAS

Love begins when a person feels another person's needs to be as important as his own.

—HARRY STACK SULLIVAN

Introduction

There are new stirrings in Christianity today. Something is going on. Evidence for that statement is found in many different places, and this is one of the problems. The evidence is in so many different places and takes so many different forms that it is difficult to know precisely what is happening. Do the stirrings have anything in common? Many different claims are being made in the name of Christ and the Spirit.

One thing which might be said is that common longings and needs of human beings are making themselves known. Such a statement may be true, but numbers of people offer themselves as proof that more must be said than that. Human longings and needs *met* and superabundantly *satisfied* is the testimony for which many lives are offered. Claims are being made about answers, not just questions.

Individual testimonies to the freedom of new life in the Spirit are now increasingly heard in the larger and more established churches and denominations. Institutional Christianity is beginning to discover unusually convinced and ex-

1

cited individuals within itself. Other marks of rebirth are found outside the more established churches in loosely organized sects and cults.

The general movement of which I am speaking has caused a glow of confused but hopeful anticipation on the part of many leaders of the established churches. They sense that something is about to shake the institutional church for good, but they do not yet know very certainly what it is and cannot make plans as if it were already an accomplished fact. Looking at the churches as a whole, one sees only ripples here and there. Reports of shifting winds have come in but as yet there is nothing of sufficient force or direction for all to discern.

In fact, in certain aspects the events noted above are disquieting. Attitudes dogmatically voiced in some sects and cells within the churches are narrow and simplistic, "rawly fundamental," and anti-intellectual. There are those who, in the name of Jesus Christ, are seeking to escape the world through "conversion." They take the historical Christ, remove him from the fullness of his working in time, and try to make him everything at the moment. Such a grasping of Christ at the moment is bound to fail in the long run for the simple reason that "the long run" is not a moment. One has only to wait, and the enthusiasm of a moment will pass. In a number of instances members of the "movement" have been called "spiritual elitists," "brittle," and "comfortably regressive." The certitude of some enthusiasts in the world seems possible only as an inverse manifestation of the world's basic fright.

To sum up: There are both possible encouragement and danger in the events we are witnessing. Will the stirrings now claimed for the Spirit amount to no more than an ephemeral, passing fad—little more, if anything, than one aspect of a cultural, psychological, or sociological syndrome? I think they *are* more, and can be more, if they feed a recognition of the importance of living Christianity as a *truly* personal religion. Man is a person; to have a religion as personal as himself is a requirement of his being. Persons may have fads, but there is no fad in the existence of persons. They are the source of fads and thus beyond their products. Persons are here to stay, and there remains much to be discerned about their nature, needs, and nurture. Still, we presently understand man's nature as a person with a fullness denied to previous generations; the application of these insights to Christianity may yield the stability needed for a significant religious life without destroying the excitement and dynamism equally important to it—an excitement and dynamism many claim to be newly discovering today. The application of such insights to the Christian life is one purpose of this book.

I must be frank at the beginning. I think reality is basic, so I try not to lose sight of it. Reality is the key to human consolation because it determines what we have to be consoled to and what there is to be consoled by. Reality is the one thing people can live with, because they *have* to live with it. What alternative is there? This is not to deny that many try to escape it and get their consolation elsewhere, but it does suggest that their flight is real and that its nature is always determined by real conditions which lie beyond it. One way or another, reality must be acknowledged; it is the only thing we can live with—yet many people feel that they cannot. This is a problem which any decent religion should help to solve.

These pages offer an attempt to be radically experiential in religion. That remark must not mislead the reader, however, for it is not my intention either to equate feeling with religion or to write a book of popular psychology. Our concern here is with the Christian religion, but it is not suggested that a person can feel his way into Christianity; in fact, the notable masters of Christian living through the centuries have to a man warned us not to depend on emotion in our religious lives.

Yet Christianity makes a difference in a person's whole life; it leaves no part of his being untouched, and so its presence can be felt. Many people feel the absence of God in their lives, which means that his presence should be recognized by feeling too.

"Feeling" as I shall use it is a synonym for experience rather than for emotion; it refers to the pervasive, immediate awareness everyone has that his experience is his own. Anything meaningful for man must ultimately draw the content of its meaning from his experience; what is totally foreign to him is totally meaningless. By that criterion there is no doubt that, in spite of the new-found enthusiasm mentioned above, many other people today feel that religion is foreign to their lives; as a result, they say it has become meaningless to them. Religion without experiential content is an empty shell, and if the shell—institutional religion—is all a person has left, he should indeed want to get rid of it as quickly as possible. Neglect of the institution or only an institutional recognition of it will do equally well the job of dismissal, although the first is the more honest alternative.

I was on a program a few years ago with a psychiatrist who told me during the course of the day that he had been raised in the church and had frequently attended two services on Sunday during his youth. He went on to say that he no longer attended church, and found more religious satisfaction in his relations with his clients than he had ever found in church services. So much so that he even scheduled therapy sessions with his clients for early Sunday morning—earlier than he would have to get up if he were still going to church!

If religion is anything, it is a personal activity. If one's life and activities in the church are less than personal, it must be said that they are less than religious. Religion involves personal presence; with that in mind, it is easy to see how the psychiatrist could have a more personally fulfilling experience with his clients than in a formal church service. Ritual is meant to be an expression of personal presence; if it is not the expression of a presence which goes before it, so to speak, it may in fact just as easily debar one from such presence as lead one to it.

We are concerned here about personal presence and the role it plays in religion. This study is an attempt to show, on the one hand, that religion begins in such presence, and on the other, that personal presence is the most fundamental constituent of our experience. In this regard, my position is the exact opposite of that described by the well-known psychologist Abraham Maslow, who has written that it is "increasingly developing that leading theologians, and sophisticated people in general, define their god, not as a person, but as a force, a principle, a gestalt-quality of the whole of Being, an integrating power that expresses the unity and therefore the meaningfulness of the cosmos, the 'dimension of depth,' etc."[1] I contend that personal presence is the only sufficient source for the meaning and existence of the universe that a sophisticated person can accept. Only a personal God can be sufficiently different from us to account for the unity, integration, and meaning that Maslow acknowledges in the universe. To deny the primacy of a personal God in favor of an impersonal principle or power seems the ultimate naïveté.

When I said a few moments ago that it was my intention to be radically experiential in religion, I meant that the purpose here is to show where, and how immediately, God can be recognized in our lives. He is experientially present to us, but in a dimension of our awareness which we are unable to translate into clear concepts. The presence of God as a Person to us cannot be conceptualized because he is the source of all meaning, but I shall maintain that he can somehow be experienced as that source.

In the end, all the activities of man that vie and compete with each other for his time, whether poetry or physics, swimming or Sanskrit, are instances of his experience competing with itself. Whatever satisfaction a person gets from any activity is an experiential satisfaction, and it is because of the satisfaction he derives from the activity that he is motivated to continue it. The approach to Christianity I am suggesting, by stressing its experiential nature, emphasizes the motivating force of Christianity in the world. Motivations can only be combated with motivations—i.e., with experience that makes a difference. Motivation cannot be resisted or improved by ideas alone. To be able to reduce the Christian option to choice between ideas is to have totally lost the essence of Christianity. All ideas in the end reflect some experiential satisfaction. Christianity, I shall try to show, reveals experientially something about our experience as a whole; thus its presence uniquely affects that experience as a whole. Wherever Christianity is found, it moves men to change the world. Knowledge and intellection play an essential role in the Christian religion, but they do so in the service of something that is more than they. If the "more" is lost, all is lost, and the first step has yet to be taken. The secret of Christianity is always to walk in the direction of its first step, for its first step is an answer to a call beyond us.

The experiential approach to Christianity presented here speaks, I believe, to an area of primary concern in our day. The term "future shock" has been coined by Alvin Toffler to describe the stress and disorientation induced in people when they are unable to adapt adequately to the rate of change to which they are exposed in the world. People suffer this when they are overwhelmed by change, and there is no doubt that many are so overwhelmed today. Confusion, defensiveness, dismay, reaction, anxiety, fear, and shallowness —all caused by rapid change—surround us.

It is not sufficient to study change from afar, from an historical point of view, according to Toffler; change, he states, must be considered in the individual, subjective lives of those who experience it, for that is where many of its most startling effects are taking place. The results of such a study indicate that man needs help in coming to terms with the future, that a new theory of adaptation to the world is called for, and that a new human accomodation to change is necessary. When it occurs too quickly in our lives—when the "future" arrives too soon—we are disoriented in the present. Such disorientation is now beginning to manifest itself in the lives of nations as well as of individuals.

Toffler writes: "We have in our time released a totally new social force—a stream of change so accelerated that it influences our sense of time, revolutionizes the tempo of daily life, and affects the very way we 'feel' the world around us. We no longer 'feel' life as men did in the past. And this is the ultimate difference, the distinction that separates the truly contemporary man from all others. For this acceleration lies behind the impermanence—the transience—that penetrates and tinctures our consciousness, radically affecting the way we relate to other people, to things, to the entire universe of ideas, art and values."[2] We should notice Toffler's emphasis on feeling, the experiential dimension I have already stressed. Accelerated change is making man feel uneasy in the world; the way we "feel life" determines our whole orientation to reality, and men are presently uneasy about life at the feeling level. Religion, as we shall consider it, deals directly with the area of malaise highlighted by Toffler's analysis.

World reorientation—orientation on a grand scale—is a great personal need in our time. To be creative in the face of change and the future requires personal security and stability, but where can these be found? We need a source of stability capable of grounding us in meaning, yet of moving us into the future as our home and refuge in the name of the very meaning it establishes.

If, as I hope to show, personal presence is the most fundamental constituent of our human experience, that presence, I suggest, provides a context within which change and the future can be met as friends and not as enemies. In that context man can begin to feel at ease with change and the future; he will find the experiential assurance that he is becoming more himself, not less, as he comes to grips with change and anticipates the future. He will realize that ultimate meaning comes out of the future, but from a source which so transcends the future that it also both permeates the present and draws on the past. Thus man's whole relation to time will be vitalized and given new meaning. Time itself will be given a perspective, and in it will furnish men with better perspectives. Every one of its dimensions—past, present, and future—will be seen to help constitute man as a person.

Something big is going on in the world today, and all human beings, especially Christians, should be taking their decisive part in the process. But to play such roles, people must be able to recognize what they are to do, and feel secure enough to do it. There are no social or individual roles without an accompanying personal experience. The examination of an experience that will lead men to their full lives in the changing world is our concern in this volume. In Part I, "The Structure," we will consider the structure of human experience, with a brief description of how man is placed in the world and how, while he is in the world, he can know a God who is absolutely different from himself. This presentation will not be elaborate, but it will locate our approach to God and religion in the contemporary scene. In Part II, "A Different God and a Different Religion," the task will be to develop the practical consequences that follow from this position. I shall try to show how the "different" God we meet in Part I influences a person's life, and in doing so, shall attempt to indicate what the presence of a different God does to such themes as creation, the temporal nature of life, body-meaning, the way we act, and the peace we seek.

In all that is here attempted, I shall try to show how the proper understanding of God as a person and proper relating to him as a person add to the Christian life—at one and the same time—an enduring structure and a consuming dynamism. A personal religion with a personal God can offer nothing less.

Notes

1. Abraham H. Maslow, *Religions, Values, and Peak-Experiences* (Columbus: Ohio State University Press, 1964), p. 55.

2. Alvin Toffler, *Future Shock* (Bantam Books: New York, 1971), p. 17.

PART ONE

The Structure

Summary

The world is primary. Man is in the world through his body, but he is more than his body in personal presence. The source of all meaning is the personal presence of a speaker. God is personal presence as the source of all the meaning of the universe. As presence God is uniquely known through human presence, entering man's life with an experiential assurance which is real but too immediate for words adequately to express.

.1.

Personal Presence
in the World

We must start with the world, for that is where we are. Truly to start with the world, however, we must start with our most basic involvement in it; that is to say, we must start with the most immediate experience of it that is possible for us. Such experience presents us with a world we perceive without effort, prior to thought—one we sink into when we relax and let ourselves go, one we arise out of precisely because we can sink into it. The world which is most fundamental in my life receives me in the form of my bed when I fall exhausted upon it at night; it is a world whose solid extension receives my body because I am of one kind with it. The release I am offered at such moments is that of like meeting like; I am received into my own. This world is the one we know through the satisfaction of eating, the world we eagerly put into our mouths while watching football games and crunch with our teeth between cheers. It is the world in which we do more for our creativity by taking a shower and feeling clean than we do by telling ourselves that concentration alone will get our job done.

All our understanding begins in a world to which we belong because we feel ourselves to be part of it. Its certainty cannot be lost; it enters into our constitution and helps define our being. The threatened loss of this world is a major element in our fear of death. What could a life be like which is not lived on solid footing? Our utmost certainty is always found in a concrete world, a place and location, not in abstract thought or universal principle. The concreteness of the world feeds us; but the abstractness of principles eats at us. The security and release the world offers me is the immediacy and effortlessness of its presence to me. It is not something I need concentrate upon to enter; instead, it helps present me to myself.

This world we are describing is one to which we naturally belong; it is one in which we feel we are a member—we do not see it from afar as if we were pure spectators. It is the world we inhabit when we stretch our arms and legs and bodies after sitting through a long lecture, and in which we show our joy by jumping and express ourselves through dancing. Through our bodies we *are* a location and we *are* space in the world; we do not just fill space as furniture does a room. As we live our bodies we organize space and extend a lifestyle beyond us into the world through the activities we initiate and by the way we react to the world and the actions of others in it. More of all this in a later chapter; for the present we need only note that whatever we do in the world creates waves that go beyond us, influencing other people and the physical fabric of the universe itself.

The bodies we live as members of the world are not just objects in that world; they happen to be our special—and only—means of knowing what any object in the world is like. On first hearing, nothing seems easier to perceive than the relations of objects to each other—what can be difficult about understanding that books are on the shelf, houses are in the block, money is in my pocket, or the ball is on the lawn? Obviously, most people have no difficulty in comprehending the simple relationships of objects around them to each other.

Normally we do not ask ourselves how we are able to know such objective relations so easily. However, if we do, do we not find that it is because we ourselves *are* bodies? From the lived experience of our bodies comes our ability to understand the relations of bodies beyond us. We know what it is for a rocket to be behind Jupiter or for a rug to be on a floor because we know what it is for a chair to be behind *us* or for a quilt to be on *us*. Upon thoughtful examination, we discover that it is only through the mediation of the bodies we are that we can understand the relations of bodies outside of us to each other. Maurice Merleau-Ponty maintained that, as far as man's understanding of the universe is concerned, *here* is the key to *there:* my understanding of my body is the key to my understanding of bodies and places beyond me—or to say the same thing in more striking terms: I am somehow everywhere by being here. If a person were not himself through his body, he would in effect be nowhere, and so he would not know what it means to be *here.*

No human person can be an unlocated "universal spectator" of the world, no matter how broad he thinks his vision is; he is always located by his body within the world he sees. The immediacy and thoroughness of our belonging to the physical world through our bodies is strikingly shown when Merleau-Ponty remarks that the visible fills and occupies me "only because I who see it do not see it from the depths of nothingness, but from the midst of itself; I the seer am also visible."[1]

Thus the experiential oneness we feel with the world through our bodies may be stressed. Other thinkers have felt an identity with the world and universe beyond them from

different points of view. The fact that man appears at a certain time in the evolution of the universe shows his identity
with the universe at a different level of analysis from that of
Merleau-Ponty. The noted anthropologist Loren Eiseley has
stated that "we are all potential fossils still carrying within
our bodies the crudities of former existences."[2] The calcium
of our bones is our kinship with the sea, and our backbones
our kinship with the reptiles. Eiseley suggests that a person
has not met himself until he catches the reflection from the
eye of an animal that is not human. There is a kinship of all
life, which goes a long way toward explaining man's fondness
for pets. Religious as well as secular men acknowledge their
identification with the physical universe. It is commonly
known that the word "human" comes from the Latin word
for earth, but the name "Adam" also has such a reference,
coming from the Hebrew word for earth. "Adam" can be
translated "earthling." The Hebrews did not just think that
man is on the earth; they knew that he is of the earth, coming
from it and returning to it.

By means of our bodily incorporation in the world we
participate in the universal extension of the physical world
beyond us. That extension is a type of absolute in the sense
that there can be, as far as our present experience is concerned, absolutely nothing physical beyond it. Nothing
physical exists outside the universe; thus every physical reality we now know is included in one totality. No absolute
differences are found among physical things insofar as they
are physical; they are distinguished from each other in terms
of relative opposition within a universal frame of reference.
From the point of view of my own experience—the basis of
everything meaningful to me—all the physical objects of the
universe are defined by the lines of spatial inclusion radiating
outward from my body. A frequently used illustration of this
fact is taken from our relation to the sun. Even though we
know that the planets of our solar system—including the

earth—revolve around the sun, for each of us the sun is always "out there." The world of our experience centers in our bodies, not in the star that centers our planetary system. Even our understanding of galaxies we have not yet seen or discovered depends upon our extending to them the perception of being and place we derive from our own bodies.

As a member of the physical universe through my body, I have something in common with the universe as a whole and all other men within it. We have observed how that universe receives me as its own when I fall upon my bed at night and when I chew and swallow it as food. But I am not just a body falling upon another body, nor a piece of matter that has smaller pieces of matter placed in a small opening called an oral cavity. I am a conscious person lying down on a bed or eating food; the satisfaction I get from eating and resting wells up within me as enjoyment that is specifically mine. Here we see a break in the continuity and sameness previously discerned in the physical universe. The consciousness I have of my enjoyment separates me from the physical elements of the universe and distinguishes me from other men, giving me something that is "especially mine" even though it depends on the physical sameness permeating the universe. My enjoyment of the physical universe is mine, but it is rooted in the "beyond me" which I share with others and upon which, with them, I depend. As members of the physical universe all men have a dependence on the "same," but the enjoyment that arises from this dependence differentiates them from each other.

The fundamental role which being-in-the-world-through-our-bodies plays in our personal lives can be simply and convincingly demonstrated by the role played by prepositions in our thought. Such terms as *in, between, over, under, behind, within, without, beyond, beside,* are basic to our thinking, but they come to us from an experience of the world which is prior to thought—the world of our personal embodiment.

Prepositions arise from our preconceptual bodily relation to the world. Only bodies can be between, in, over, under, or behind each other in a literal sense. It is a mark of the primacy of bodily location in our orientation to reality that, even when we are speaking of such abstract things as ideas and theories, we say that one of them falls between two others, that one idea is contained within another, or that a theory is beyond our concern—in addition to being beside the point.

It is not my purpose to give an exhaustive analysis at this time of our membership in the world through our bodies. I hope enough has been said, however, to establish beyond doubt that we *are* so related to the world. For being in the world through a body determines how I am able to express myself in the world. The necessary use of prepositions in my thought is a case in point. But in any adequate analysis of man's life, we must recognize that he is more than a bodily location. He is also a personal presence reaching beyond his body.

When we think of man as *what* is located in the universe instead of *how* he is located, we emphasize the way he transcends his body through personal presence. Man's presence in the world is always rooted in and located through his body, but it goes beyond his body. In this dimension of his being, I shall try to show that the *absolutely other* becomes meaningful. Man as a person confronts every other person as an "absolutely other" in which he cannot participate, in contrast to the elemental sameness of the physical universe in which he does participate.

When we think of otherness we usually think of it in terms of a negative opposition to ourselves; we tend to think of it, in other words, simply as "not me." But the attempt to describe personal confrontation by such opposition does not do justice to the facts. We know the otherness of another person not just as the negation of ourselves; another person is a positive source of revelation who can burst upon us and challenge us by his being. In so doing he shatters the intellectual complacency of our merely negative way of thinking about him. If, for example, I think of another person only as the negation of myself, I will rob him of his positive reality as a person so effectively that he will never be able to challenge me in a confrontation. He will not be able to say to me anything *different* from what I wish to say to myself.

The difference from each other with which we are confronted in personal presence even has roots in our sensual enjoyment of the world. Such enjoyment, as I indicated a moment ago, is a source of egoism in our lives, for sensory satisfaction considered in itself is a positive activity which cannot be shared with another person. It is uniquely mine. You cannot enjoy my dessert, and I cannot enjoy the refreshment you feel while playing in the surf. The separate world in which each person is immersed and which he feels for himself helps to establish his identity as an incommunicable ego, a center of experience absolutely different from all other men. The different being each one of us knows himself to be through his immediate experience requires that we respect other persons as an "other than we" in a positive rather than just a negative sense. The presence of another person in his otherness is our singular experience of radical difference in the world.

Another dimension of a person's otherness from us is his infinity. This seeming contradiction is explored below, and will be found, I believe, to be perfectly cogent. The relation of otherness and infinity to our ability to exhaust the reality of another person by our thought of him is most important for understanding the nature of personal presence and our relation to God as persons. Because it is an analytic sort of topic, I am setting it off as a section (to p. 22) which the reader may skip if he prefers and is not much philosophically in-

clined. Yet it is in certain ways fundamental to the completeness of this presentation.

I should like at this point to indicate briefly that the presence of two people to each other as persons overflows opposition in the manner in which we are able intellectually to
conceive of opposition. Personal presence, I believe, involves
a conscious dimension too immediate and full to be repre-
sented in intellectual terms at all. And that is the dimension
of our experience in which religion begins.

There is something about personal presence which
reaches beyond anything the mind can conceive; this aspect
has been called by Emmanual Levinas the infinity of personal presence. At its simplest, according to Levinas, such
infinity may be defined as *that which cannot be contained in
a totality.* A person is infinite, in other words, in the sense
that his presence cannot be finally summed up, totaled, or
capped. It always exists beyond the last thing said. What
cannot be contained in a totality necessarily overflows clear
definition or representation, for it cannot be seized for what
it is in any limited way. We thus cannot have a clear idea of
it. The infinite, per se, cannot be systematized or completely
charted.

If we accept the definition of infinity as "that which overflows thought," its meaning converges with another concept
we have been using, that of otherness. We have observed
that another person is radically other—absolutely other—
than I am. Otherness which is "absolute" is otherness taken
in the strict sense of "to be the other." We must go slowly
here to get the significance of this distinction, but the care
exercised in acquiring the insight will be more than repaid
by its consequences in our lives. The other whose formal
characteristic is "to be other" necessarily resists inclusion in
a totality, for if it *shared* inclusion in the same totality with

others it would no longer be "the other." To know otherness for what it is, then, is necessarily not to be systematized with it. A person is able to be the absolutely other because he is infinite: he cannot be adequately conceived as a mere member of a totality within thought.

In fact a person, as absolute other, cannot even be thought of as composing a totality with thought itself. Personal presence transcends thought; it is too much for thought alone to handle. The relation of otherness between persons transcends the type of relations with which logic, as an intellectual discipline, can deal. Now we can understand why the "absolutely other" and the "infinite" coincide in this anaylsis. To say a person is "absolutely other" and "infinite" is simply to say that a person, and thus personal presence, overflows thought.

Infinity is, by definition, the other, the more. Infinity is not an abstract idea; it is a kind of being. Levinas' way of putting it is to say that "the idea of infinity is the mode of being, the *infinition*, of infinity," which is to say that knowledge of infinity is by means of the infinity of one's own being.[3] I know the infinite through an immediate experience of my own infinitude—not by an act of my intellect alone. Experiencing my own infinity, I realize that I am more than even I can clearly think about myself. I am more than any totality of my acts, for there is some dimension of my being which, although expressing itself through my acts, is always beyond them.

Because of the infinitude of my being, I can question the meaning of both myself and the universe as they are totalities, asking what their ultimate meaning is, asking what they are *for*. Simply to ask the question, "What is that for?" requires a prior recognition of something beyond the object questioned. To be able to ask a question about anything is always to be distinguished from the thing asked about, because we must be beyond something in order to look at it or turn back upon it. The "I" which I am, in questioning the meaning of my being, always stands beyond the "I" I can grasp as an object of my thought. The "I" I most intimately am, the "questioning I," seeks meaning because it is a source of meaning beyond all the objects of the world. That "I" is the infinitude I experience in myself when I go beyond my past self in response to the loving presence of another person. To be able to wonder about oneself and the universe is to be beyond oneself and the universe. A person is always beyond himself; that is his definition. It is also the basis of his positive experience of infinity and of his longing for God.

This brings us to another aspect of personal presence which we must consider. It does not require deep analysis to understand, but is of the utmost importance in our lives: I am referring to the relation of personal presence to the meaning we search for in the world. Man lives by meaning; a meaningless life is a worthless life, but in spite of the value of meaning to us, most people have trouble in accounting for its origin. Indeed, many persons seldom think of its origin at all; the topic seems to be one reserved for specialists called philosophers. For centuries philosophers have asked about "the meaning of meaning," but this is not a subject which should be restricted to them. The origin of meaning is a topic for everyone who wants to make sense of his life in the world, for no one can do without meaning. Where does it come from? What is the ultimate source of significance in the world?

Think of two persons present to each other. Have they ever said the last thing they can say? No. No matter what or how much they have said in the past, they can always say something more. In fact, personal presence is the source of our "idea" of infinity because when two people are present to each other they can always say more than they have said in the past. Even if they happen to use the same words, they can say something new simply by choosing to use the words again. "I love you," is new each time two lovers whisper it. No matter what one person has already said, as long as he remains present with me he can justify and interpret his words in a new way by saying something more. His presence is an inexhaustible source of meaning and thus a final guarantee of what he says.

I have just said that personal presence is a source of meaning. On the analysis of such presence given here, it must be claimed that it is not just *a* source of meaning in the world; it is the only sufficient source of all meaning.

Before going further we must examine the nature of meaning considered just in itself. Where do we find it? What makes it significant to us? We find meaning in the world and we find it in other people, but the meaning we find in persons has an ultimacy about it which makes it the only sufficient source of the meaning we find in the world. Man is an animal who speaks, and speaking, we shall see, is the source of meaning. Our silence and even the silence of the world achieve their significance only from our expectation of speech. What can the *silence* of the world mean apart from speech? Silence can be disappointing only because of what is not said, a disappointment made possible because something could be said. Fear of deception by the world is also possible only within the setting of speech, for it is by words that hypocrisy and deceit are accomplished. Deception is a perversion of communication.

Do we not say when something is especially meaningful to us, "It speaks to me?" When, on the other hand, a painting or a musical composition is meaningless to us we comment, "It doesn't say anything to me." Both modes of expression are obviously personal, for only persons speak in the formal sense of the word. If we think about it, we will discover that every experience we have of the world, or of anything within the world, as other—as something that can say something to us —depends upon our prior acceptance of the other as a self-sufficient speaker.

A mother playing with her child makes the child's toys speak to him; by so doing she actualizes and develops the child's expectancy of a conversational relationship with the objects of his room and ultimately with the whole world. "Bad chair to let Billy fall off—don't do that again!" and "Billy, say good night to Teddy Bear,"—such behavior gives Billy a dialogical orientation toward the world, but an orientation that depends upon the primordial presence of his mother to him. It is the presence of his mother—always of some other person—that lets the world be what it is for him. We know persons before things and things through persons.

When we say of some object that it has "meaning in itself," we are actually saying that it has a meaning which everyone can recognize. The "in itself" of the meaning in actual fact indicates the availability of the meaning to other people in a human community. Man never confronts a "bare world"; he confronts the world through words he has learned from others. He thus confronts a world that has been thematized by men. The vocabulary a person has at his disposal to describe the world assures that the world he describes will be a human, culturally conditioned one. The world does speak to us, but it can be made to say different things at different times; the approach we take to it in science and art determines to a large extent what the world can say about itself to us. If we look at the world through a microscope, we will not see a landscape; a hand says something different in a painted portrait than it does in an X ray; winter means one thing to a farmer and another to a skier. But even when the world does reveal itself, the otherness we find within it is relative. Its otherness is always found within a totality; no object in the physical universe says anything absolutely different to us from any other object. In fact, one of the most striking lessons science teaches us about the universe is the sameness of the atomic and chemical constitution of the galaxies that extend throughout its heavens.

Wherever we find meaning it satisfies us because it limits anarchy; it destroys chaos and indifference. Meaning prohibits the arbitrary because meaning is the presence of something that commands and calls. We can reason deductively because meaning commands consequences, and we can listen to it because it calls. But limiting the arbitrary requires the presence of something that is not arbitrary. Something must exist which of itself limits alternatives to it. Meaning answers our needs and gives us security for precisely that reason: it gives us location in the sense of denying arbitrary alternatives. A human person, we have seen, is always a location; because of that, he is always a perspective. That is why the meaningful for him must be a location and a perspective too. The arbitrary and indecisive will not do; they contradict the nature of man's fundamental insertion into reality through his body.

What source can supply the characteristics of the meaningful just described? Once more we discover the answer to be personal presence.

The presence of another person makes us want to talk and makes us feel obliged to explain ourselves. If I think I am doing something alone and suddenly discover that someone has been watching me, I feel compelled to speak. The presence of another person can question me so completely that my whole world is challenged; I may even feel the need to justify my previously arbitrary enjoyment of the physical universe. Why do I use time the way I do? What is important to me? Why do I treat others the way I do? Personal presence demands and elicits meaning from me when I feel myself located before it.

By calling us into question, the presence of another is the source of our creativity, for it is by having to explain ourselves—or something we know—to another that we *must* go beyond ourselves. In the searching presence of another I feel obliged to express myself, and so I become myself anew through the world in response to him. Expressing myself in the world I help create the world by making physical reality say more than it has in the past. The reason I avoid others is so that I will not have to become new.

We never know what we can do until we are called upon to do it. We do not know what we know until we try to explain it; by explaining and expressing ourselves we actually learn something about ourselves for the first time, for we are more ourselves with others than we can be alone. It is the common experience of those who teach that they learn by teaching; they do not first learn and then teach. One can memorize and then repeat what he has memorized, but that is neither learning nor teaching. Are we not all sometimes astonished to hear ourselves say what the presence of another has solicited from us?

The presence of another is able to challenge the meaning of my life just because I recognize the person who confronts me to be himself a source of meaning. How that can be the case is illustrated by a conversation in which I recently participated.[4] At that time a friend told me that he no longer read the books of a certain well-known philosopher of communication because the latter had said in an interview that he didn't believe his own work; it was all a joke. The remark may have been facetious, but the person to whom I was talking said, "There is a man who is supposed to be an expert on communication, and he doesn't stand behind his own words." The suggestion that he would not stand behind his words made those words meaningless to one of his earlier readers. Why pay attention to such a man? Meaning is the presence of something, and its finality comes from the type of presence it manifests. The only presence that can be ultimately significant is an infinite one, one that cannot be exhausted or relativized. Meaning, we have seen, speaks to us, but the ultimate significance of speech arises from the fact that a speaker remains present in it to interpret his own signs from a source which, by definition, can never be totally expressed.[5] Meaningfulness ultimately originates only because something can be volunteered from a locatable but inexhaustible source who will not abandon his words.

To make our point clear, let us imagine a situation in which no ultimate meaning could be found. If everything real were contained without remainder in one plane of being, no ultimate meaning could be discovered within that plane because every individual within it could, with equal justice, be seen from the arbitrary point of view of any other individual. There would thus be no possibility of any individual standing behind what he said. Nothing in the plane would be absolutely different from anything else; nothing would be privileged. As a consequence, nothing would be uniquely itself or singular; all meaning within the plane would lack finality. But a person, we have seen, is not a plane figure which can adequately be known from external points of view alone. A person is something in himself; he is an inexhaustible source of activity who cannot be formalized and contained in a totality; he is a presence which makes a unique demand upon others in his own name. That, in fact, is precisely why a person is named. He has a proper name because he is properly something in himself.

Meaning must have a source, a "place" of origin, a beginning, because it is the opposite of the arbitrary. That is why an infinite regress can never be a source of meaning; such a regress is the infinite postponement of meaning rather than meaning's origin. Meaning begins with the presence of a Gestalt or whole in relation to which particular things become meaningful. The basic world-attitudes of people may vary from person to person (which is the reason we say that people live in different worlds), but the possible differences

among such world-attitudes must not distract us from the
presence as presence of the persons who project them. The
beginning of all meaning is the infinitude of personal presence itself.

Meaning in our lives begins with the presence of another
person, our mother or someone playing the mother role.
Other types of presence soon enter the picture, that of the
father, for example, and then frequently that of a brother of
sister; but without the felt presence of another person
through physical touching and audible speaking the normal
development of a child is impossible. When a child is not
wanted and the presence offered him is neither personal nor
genuine, the basic sense of the goodness and meaningfullness
of life is lost. Security is destroyed, and the ability to accept
reality for what it is is impaired. Many parents who have
never been truly present to their children—who have
treated them as objects or strangers to be bought off with
allowances and privileges—make a show of giving them a
meaningful life, but the meaning offered is always objective
and externally forced upon the proposed recipient. Such parents try to give their children meaning, but they have never
made themselves available in a significantly personal way to
their children as a source of meaning. That can be done only
through the personal exposure we call presence, and it takes
time, something such parents do not have for their children.
Under such circumstances, the rebellion of youngsters
against their parents is not the shameful spectacle it is often
pictured to be by undiscerning conventional society. If we
have learned anything from depth psychology it is the forgotten Christian truth that we must not judge others on the basis
of external appearance alone. The rebellion of young people
is often no more than a disguised cry for help. It is a sign that
life and hope remain, for it is actually a quest, a testing, a
search for the presence which has been missing from their
lives.

As we mature, we discover that meaning adequate to reality exceeds the ability of human presence to account for it. Human beings die, and both the extent and age of the physical universe surpass human resources. Accordingly, if our lives and the being of the universe are to be ultimately meaningful, we realize that we must live in a presence adequate to explain the universe in its totality and capable of overcoming death. Needing a presence that can be the Source of all meaning, we are led to acknowledge God in our lives—the topic of our next chapter.

Notes

1. Maurice Merleau-Ponty, *The Visible and the Invisible,* ed. Claude Lefort, trans. Alphonso Lingis (Evanston: Northwestern University Press, 1968), p. 113.

2. Loren Eiseley, *The Immense Journey* (New York: Vantage Books, 1957), p. 6.

3. Emmanuel Levinas, *Totality and Infinity: An Essay on Exteriority,* trans. Alphonso Lingis (Pittsburg: Duquesne University Press, 1969), p. 26. I am much indebted to this book.

4. The conversation, interestingly enough, exactly parallels a part of the presentation of Levinas in the work just cited.

5. Cf. Levinas, *op. cit.,* pp. 91 and 98.

.2.

God as Presence

If consensus were to be sought among contemporary views on the nature of God, there is no doubt that agreement would be found on the statement that God is not an object. The denial of objectivity, as over against a denial of the reality of God, is so widely accepted and argued today that I need not restate the case in detail here. Suffice it to say that the thrust of this view is to deny that God is *a* being, an object, standing over and against his creation in a purely external manner. We owe the contemporary stress on this insight to man's increased interest in the knowing process. If God were an object, he would have the same kind of being as objects in the world; consequently he could be known in the same way as those objects. But nothing could be further from the truth; even Scripture tells us that no man has ever seen God. (John 1:18)

The religious person finds himself in a paradoxical situation: he needs a God who can be known as the world is known—that is, with the same type of conviction; but he needs a different kind of God from one who could be known in that way! We need a God who can save us as well as be known by us, but to save us, God must be basically different from us.

The first thing we must say about God (and this is a traditional insight) is that he is different from us; we can view a good deal of contemporary theology as an exercise in how that difference can be meaningfully described. Even to call God "the supreme Being" seems to objectify him and set him apart in an illicit way for some theologians. In addition, any idea of objectivity in the nature of God carries static connotations offensive to contemporary man's awareness of the dynamic, evolutionary nature of reality. If God is the full perfection of Being, already accomplished and complete, existing objectively by himself apart from the universe, what is the point of the world history—indeed the cosmic history —in which we are caught up? If world history is nothing but the acting out of a play entitled *Providence,* the script for which God has already completed, it is said that men count for nothing. Such a view of history contradicts the need we feel for significance in our lives and destroys our hope of making genuine contributions to the development of man. A naïve, mechanical, and inhuman view of reality results from any religion that would knowingly or unknowingly accept God as a mere object.

The approach to God I am rather suggesting is through our experience of personal presence in this world. The infinitude of such presence we found to be the only sufficient source of meaning in the world, for only such a presence can be self-justifying. It is a source of meaning in its own right and thus demands respect. Because of that fact, personal infinitude cannot be known by purely external observation and from points of view arbitrarily related to it. It must reveal itself.

We find the primacy of the absolutely other in our lives as a source of, and demand for, meaning in the world; but, as mentioned above, our need for meaning exceeds the meaning for which human presence can account. The physical immensity of the evolving universe and the thorough destructiveness of death threaten human meaning in its entirety. Thus led by considerations of the basic role of the other in our lives, we discover the need for an Other who is basic to all reality. God is the Other whose presence gives meaning to the universe as a whole and whose presence can save man from annihilation in death.

Everyone finds himself in an odd situation when he tries to conceive of God. Actually, our concept of God cannot be a concept at all—a condition we have already found to apply to the "concept" of infinity. If it is God who is known, a relationship more complete than anything the intellect could supply by means of concepts would be the only "proper" way to know him.

A disposition of our whole being is required in our knowledge of God; a reference prior to—because more basic than —our objective way of thinking. That realization is the truth grasped by theologies which will not allow God to be thought of as an object. A God who had to be known in a more intimate way than we know external objects could not be conceptual or play a "merely verbal" role in our lives. Efficacious belief in such a God, belief that makes a difference, would be possible, for the only possible recognition of him would be personally full and moving. We would have to know him as a personal presence calling to us or not at all. As words go, however, "person terms" are the furthest-reaching means we have at our disposal by which to refer to God; properly understood, they force us into a deeper dimension of reality than the intellectual distinctions we make in referring to external objects.

God cannot be adequately described in concepts; neither can presence. Presence, we have seen, asks something of us and demands something from us; it gives, allows, and solicits meaning. As the source of meaning, it cannot be described from outside itself. It cannot be made an object, yet it calls us to express ourselves to others through the objects at our disposal. The new comes from it because the infinitude of presence is always more than we can know or anticipate at any one moment. Above all, personal presence cannot be produced by participation; it is constituted by the "over against," the different. Persons can be themselves only with other persons, which means that absolute difference, not relative difference, is constitutive of personal being. As a person I do not so much live in another as *with* him. Love, for example, is a peculiar kind of relationship: it is a union which destroys separation but at the same time intensifies distinction. People feel more *themselves* when they are in love, even though love is a way they give themselves to another. Intensity of distinction is the source of richness in personal relationships.

All this is not to deny that there are many New Testament references to Christians living in God and in Jesus Christ. It has been said that St. Paul uses the phrase "in Christ" 164 times; the actual number may vary depending on the authorship of certain epistles, but no one can deny that the metaphor is most important to his thought. It is a way in which St. Paul and other writers of the New Testament describe the intimacy of believers with Christ. When physical metaphors are used to describe personal intimacy—such metaphors as the inclusion of the members of a living body in the body as a whole, or the inclusion of branches in a vine, to take an example from the Fourth Gospel—the "in" causes us no trouble. We must always remember, however, that personal presence itself is not physical; it transcends space and cannot properly be described in the way objects are related to each other.

Our greatest security is to live *with* God, not in him, for by being infinitely different from us he has infinite riches and

strength to share with us. Trying to live with God instead of
in him, I am at ease about my own identity and his. I know
my need, which is complete, and I know his resources, which
are Infinite. If I try to live in God, I may try to be other than
myself; if I am in him, I think to myself, why does my life not
have more of his ease? I tend to become confused about both
his identity and mine. We live *with* persons, not in them, for
persons relate to each other as the *absolutely other;* because
we are embodied persons, our most intimate relations with
each other are face-to-face relationships, not relationships of
spatial inclusion. We can live in *the presence* of another person, and there is even a sense in which we can meaningfully
speak of being "possessed" by another person's presence, but
the primacy of personal presence is clear in both cases. To
speak simply of living "in" another person, however, may
make us forget the absolute difference between persons because of the usual spatial connotation of the preposition.
There is no way we can live in God in the sense of being a
part of him.

   To live "in God" is essentially a nonspatial way in which
God is present to us. Because of the interiority of personal
being—that is to say, because personal being is deep and rich
—persons can be intimately united with each other in their
"centers"; human beings, for example, when they sit side by
side can be more united with each other than merely touching at their extremities, like two tiles on the floor. By the
same token, when human beings are united in the depths of
their being, they can be in each other's presence even
though they are miles apart. By freely willing the same thing,
persons become one with each other in the most intimate
way possible.

   We live "in" another by willing the same thing as another.
To will what God wills, to let his will which is different from
mine rule me, is the way I live "in" him. His influence in my
life is the means of my living in him, but that influence
depends upon his difference from me.

God and I, precisely because we are both somehow persons, do not form a totality. It is because God and his creatures do not form a totality that God can be their Creator.

> ... the idea of creation *ex nihilo* expresses a multiplicity not united into a totality; the creature is an existence which indeed does depend on an other, but not as a part that is separated from it. Creation *ex nihilo* breaks with system, posits a being outside of every system, that is, there where its freedom is possible. Creation leaves to the creature a trace of dependence, but it is an unparalleled dependence: the dependent being draws from this exceptional dependence, from this relationship, its very independence, its exteriority to the system.[1]

Created in the image of God, persons are those beings who, when in a group, cannot be totaled. But because persons cannot be a sum, they can be a source. Infinity, as we are considering it, is a source of new things because it is never any one thing; it is entirely different from *things*.

God is Presence who accounts for presence; his presence is known through the presence of men and cannot be known apart from theirs. Still, his presence cannot be equated with theirs. He is the Source of all meaning. But if both God and man are recognized by means of a personal presence transcending concepts, is there any way man's difference from God can be made clear? I think there is: by means of the type of location man's presence has through his body.

Man's existence in the world is so located through his body that he will never be able to play God or confuse himself with God in an absolute manner. Because there is a sense in which man is his body, and is a member of the world because of that fact, the world is the place of human expression. Man must show he is a person by organizing something beyond himself, by extending the life-style originating in his lived body beyond that body. The extension of man's life-style by the electronic nervous system of science has been pointed out by Marshall McLuhan. It is man's vocation to personalize the physical context in which he finds himself and thus make the world mean one thing rather than another. Man's world is a world of meaning, and since persons are the ultimate source of meaning only personal presence can account for his world. The world is the means by which men live together, and it is shaped by the way men make themselves available to each other in their mutual expression.

At its level, personal presence is an open-ended *experiential absolute;* as experienced, such presence is an ultimate which cannot be further qualified from outside itself in a way that adds enrichment to it. Everything in the world is relative except one thing: the otherness we experience in personal presence. That is why experiencing the presence of other people is the only key we have for recognizing the presence of God; God becomes present to us in and through their presence. To say this is not to deny that God is more than men and, as God, independent of men to the extent that he can be addressed directly. What we are saying is that presence can only be known by presence—that infinitude can only be known by infinitude. Recognizing God is not an intellectual exercise; life with God cannot be summarized in propositions.

Our concepts cannot adequately dissect and describe the infinitude with which persons are present to each other, but because presence for us is always located, expressing itself from a certain point of view, we can use that fact to distinguish the presence of God from the presence of man and the presence of different men from each other. Because the infinitude of man's presence is located for us by his body, his presence is never known apart from a specific world orientation. God as God is not so located within the world. He is Absolute Otherness, who locates both human absolute otherness and the physical universe from which that otherness lives.

An unavoidable ambiguity is found in calling presence the

ultimate source of meaning, for it both is and is not. As ours, it is not; as God's it is. But only our experience of human presence activates the mode of experience that enables us to recognize God's Presence for the category-breaking Infinity it is. Only as we live the infinitude of presence ourselves— only as we are *infinition*, to use Levinas' term—can we recognize God's presence. But so recognized, God's presence affects the wholeness of our experience and motivates us through the complete movement of our being.

The presence of God is the source of all meaningfulness. Thus wherever meaning is found in the universe, there is his presence; wherever we are called to deepen meaning, there is his presence; wherever we are called to new meaning, there is his presence. Our world exists in his presence and all change occurs within it. His is the presence we cannot leave. Meaning, then, for a Christian is not something he impersonally notes and files away; it is something he personally feels, for he recognizes through it the presence of its Source.

Meaning—all meaning—for a Christian is *call* and *motivation;* it is a life, an adventure, companionship, trust, and hope. It is personal presence. Truly to understand what the Christian tradition means by redemption, for example, is actively to be involved in changing the world; the presence of God in the presence of his meaning leaves us no alternative but to live fully with him. That is true even in the way a Christian does mathematics; he wants always to know more, and the drive both to discover and apply mathematical knowledge is a way he speaks to God. If we will feel meaning as the expression of personal presence, in addition to thinking it in an abstract way, the infinitude of Presence will constantly carry us beyond our present attainment to a future ever richer in meaning and ever more fully humane.

In summary we may say that in human presence God is immediately present to us, but not in a way that can be conceptually clarified. The infinitude of presence overwhelms our intellect, but all is not lost, for the presence of one person can be distinguished from that of another by what he says to us and by what he asks of us. Human persons ask one another questions from different points of view and speak to each other within the common context of a world structure whose meaning is rooted in their bodies. God does not speak to us just within a world structure; he speaks—that is, creates—the world structure itself. God asks us questions through human questions, but he always asks us questions beyond human questions. Another human being may question my whole being by the way he looks at me, but through him God questions me in a way that includes my questioner as well as myself. In questioning me through another person God questions the whole community of men at once.

Human persons can say something, but God, by being the ultimate answer to all questions, speaks through everything. He is Infinite in what he can say, but he is concrete and specific in what he does say to us. Because he is Presence who creates presence, and because presence by definition is that which cannot be totaled, God cannot possibly be considered the totality of human presence. Human presence is always a dependent, perspectival, conditioned presence; God is Presence whose free decision enables contingent conditions and perspectives to arise in the first place.

Christians know their lives are now lived in the presence of God. In the next chapter, I shall speak of the relation of God's presence to the Christian doctrine of creation, finally understanding that doctrine in terms of God's presence. The presence of God is the touchstone of everything Christian in the past, present, and future. In later chapters we shall examine the question of time and the special role of the future in men's lives, attempting to see how God's presence gives meaning to them; but even now we can see how a common hope and expectation of Christians stresses the primacy of God's presence in human life.

An identifying belief of Christians is their awaiting the second coming of Christ. "And he shall come again in glory" is one of the oldest creedal affirmations made about the founder of Christianity. The second coming of Christ is otherwise known as the parousia; it is what all Christians expect. I need not give a detailed exegesis of that expectation here, but it should be pointed out that *parousia*, a Greek word, means "presence." Christian belief in a Second Coming should not be confused with metaphorical and sometimes fanciful descriptions about how the Second Coming will occur: riding on clouds is not essential to the Christian doctrine. Actually, of course, no one knows precisely how Christ will come again. What we do know is that, living in the presence of God already, the only thing Christians can await is more of God's presence. God's presence is the beginning and end of man's life. The coming which is the parousia means that Christians expect God's presence to be manifested in a new way sometime in the future; that manifestation is the meaning of the future for Christians. Because the future presence of God will be in a new mode, it will be as if it were a new —and so a second—coming to us. In its newness, Christians expect God's presence in creation to be so obvious and thoroughgoing that God will then be known by all to be "all in all" (1 Cor. 15:28 AV). The sure point of the Second Coming is that God's presence only leads to his presence; existing in that presence is life for a Christian and such life can only grow, knowing no death.

The central and most basic contention of Christianity is that personal presence is the context of personal presence. Ultimate reality for a Christian is the inseparable presence of distinct Persons to each other, for that is what Christians believe God has revealed his own intimate life to be. That, in fact, is the significance of the doctrine of the Trinity. The infinite presence to each other of Persons—Father, Son, and Holy Spirit—is the ultimate source of all the meaning and all the being there is according to the Christian religion. Because the Persons mysteriously living the one life of God are Infinite and not able to be contained within a totality or system, we, from our own experience, recognize the meaningfulness of accepting them as the source of our existence and of the existence of the universe. They, and we as living in their presence, have a significance that completely transcends the present form of a universe which is described by science as running down in its totality. Life and all being are meaningful for us because of their presence. They call the kind of persons we are into existence out of their love just so that we can live with them. Creation is the call of love. The Word of the Father calls a universe into existence to be the means of communication among the kind of persons we are, persons who must grow in perfection and unity.

The Persons of the Trinity locate each other immediately by themselves without intermediating elements within which and from which they live. We, on the other hand, are located for each other by God through our bodies in the present state of the universe. But that very fact means that our highest personal calling and intimacy with God is to be present with him through the universe and through the presence of other persons with whom he has placed us. There is no other way.

Notes

1. Emmanuel Levinas, *Totality and Infinity*, p. 104.

PART II

A Different God
and a Different Religion

.3.

Creation as a Fact of Experience

The title of this Part of our discussion must not confuse us. The different God is the same we have been talking about; the different religion is historical Christianity. Christianity that is truly historical always makes a difference. In these chapters I want to discuss our relationship with the personal God of Christianity who is absolutely different from us and see how living with such a God influences our lives. Things are obviously not well in many people's religious lives, and a religion that made a significant difference to those lives would be a different religion, even if it were called by the familiar name of Christianity. Old doctrines would become new; such newness is what we hope to discover in the themes of creation, hope, body-meaning, humility, love, and peace when they are radically personalized by the God who is Presence.

Personal presence is the ingredient of life man cannot do without. Security and meaning proceed from it, and when such presence is lacking, insecurity and the threat of meaninglessness indicate our need for it. A child begins to learn about itself because of the presence of its mother; fondling, stroking, and speaking are modes of presence, and psychologists urge mothers to be present with their infants by these means as much as possible. Love has been said to be the purpose of living, but love is possible only because it is a type of presence. It is also said that man grows within religion; the statement makes sense because religion is the recognition of presence, and all growth takes place within presence.

Many people have indicated that their primary religious problem is to discover God's presence. That is the proper way to state the problem, for God cannot be *made* present; his presence can only be discovered. Such is the meaning of Gerhard Ebeling's paradoxical-sounding remark that the word of God can only be discovered in God's word: that is to say, wherever God is discovered he is discovered as already present. Pascal actually said it first, and he was right: God can be looked for only because he is present.

I have tried in Part I to indicate the ultimacy and immediacy of God's presence to us. I am now going to speak unashamedly about Christian living, and the task will be difficult. We are not used to talking about Christianity in that way. To do so puts us on the spot, for such talk assumes that a commitment has been made, that a big gamble has been taken. We are used to taking gambles and stands from time to time in our lives, but most of the time we take them only for our projects and goals; we defend them because we are their ultimate defense. But to commit ourselves unashamedly to Christianity is to take a stand about the nature of basic reality. Such a commitment must make a difference other people can see in our lives; thus it takes us off of dead center. The thought of making such an absolute decision about the Source of the cosmos may make us feel our smallness and insufficiency in a unique way. Can we make such a judgment from our limited point of view? Should we make such a judgment, we ask ourselves. The thought of it strikes us with cosmic humility; it would seem more fitting for us to lack the presumption such a judgment calls for. On that view it is lack of pride—a Christian virtue—that keeps us from being Christian.

On the other hand, it is not impossible that the change in our lives required by a firm decision about ultimate values may be doing more to keep us from religious living than our supposed inability to make a decision about ultimate reality. Unwillingness to have our lives changed, rather than humility about making a judgment, may well be our greatest religious difficulty. We do not like to change, but, as we shall see, there is no Christianity without constant change. Satisfaction with ourselves as we are may turn out to be the real origin of the "cosmic humility" we try to project. After all, everything we do implies some kind of judgment about what we think is ultimately important.

We have not yet exhausted the difficulties of talking about Christianity in a committed way. If we start where we should in our discussion we must start at the beginning, and that means with the doctrine of creation. But the Christian doctrine of creation does not mean much to many contemporary persons; they feel it is a myth inherited from the past, and that to accept it is to assume everything to begin with. The Christian doctrine of creation is thought by many people to be no more than one notion among many as to how the universe began; they thus try to reduce it to an abstract theory of cosmology, and an outdated one at that. But such an interpretation of the doctrine is not the *Christian* doctrine and certainly will not satisfy the approach we have taken to religion. In our approach, creation, like everything significantly religious, must make an experiential difference to us: it must be experientially significant in our lives now. In the early nineteenth century, Friedrich Schleiermacher also wanted to make the doctrine of creation meaningful in man's

ongoing experience, and he consequently defined the doctrine as man's feeling of absolute dependence. Schleiermacher did not use "feeling" in a narrow emotional sense,
and neither do I. His motivation has much in common with
my own, but although there is an occasional terminological
similarity between the two views, the position here is based
on a quite different analysis. As with any religious position,
however, one is glad to have an analysis corroborated by the
experience of other people in different circumstances than
one's own, anywhere in history.

I have said that many people find the Christian doctrine of
creation to be a problem; the difficulty is in fact much greater
than might be expected. Properly understood, the doctrine
is nothing less than a scandal! Since I have tried to be frank
in our discussion so far, I shall not attempt to hide the scandal
of the Christian doctrine of creation here. It is not a philosophical opinion; it is not a "teaching," a formula, the first
article of a creed, or something Christians must *say*. It is
rather the acceptance of the fact that we are loved! Loved
in a deep, personal, and intimate sense by the creating
Source of the expanding universe.

Who can realize the significance of those words? No one.
Certainly not people who are only engaged in theological
chatter. But when the awareness of the doctrine does creep
into our lives, it forces us to expression by every means at our
disposal—even words.

From New Testament times onward the proclamation of
Christianity—the Gospel—has been known as the Good
News. Firmly to maintain that we are loved in a personal way
by the Source of the cosmic grandeur extending indefinitely
beyond us scandalizes modern man by its presumption. If it
is to be known for what it claims to be, Christianity is at the
same time scandal and Good News. Its scandal is its Good
News. The greater the possibility of our realizing its scandal,
the greater the possibility of our realizing its truth; the trou-

ble with Christianity is that its news is too good. It is more than we can bear, but that fact is the only possible "proof" of its truth. Since we cannot bear it, it has to bear us, which means that it creates us. It changes us.

Christians see the creative agency of God the Father in the life and resurrection from the dead of Jesus Christ. In Jesus, the Father who is the Source of the universe reveals his radical newness within the world of man as man. To live intimately with Jesus or, to use the metaphor of St. Paul, to live "in Christ" is to be recreated. As Paul said, "if any one is in Christ, he is a new creation [creature]; the old has passed away, behold, the new has come. All this is from God, who through Christ reconciled us to himself. . . . " (2 Corinthians 5:17 f.) To be redeemed means to be recreated, that is to say, to have a new kind of complete dependence on the Father through the Son. For Christians the redemption of the world in Jesus Christ is the key to the first creation of the universe by the Father "out of nothing." The Christian testimony is that, *out of nothing* we have, the Father wills to reconcile us to himself through his Son.

The relationship between life with Christ and the creation of the universe is indicated in the biblical text quoted above, for the word Paul uses for "creation" in the passage is the same word used in Mark (10:6 and 13:19) and in 2 Peter (3:4) when explicit reference is being made to the beginning of the universe as a whole. Even the Greek word for regeneration found in Titus 3:5 literally means "to be created again."

Assured that the highly personal Christian doctrine of creation is a scandal in our day, let us pause a moment to examine our use of the word "creature" in our everyday language. Creatures derive from the act of creation, and our linguistic usage would indicate that we feel more at home with them than with the act itself.

As we currently use the word "creature," it tends to refer to something subhuman. We speak of "creatures of the deep," or of the forest, and we frequently use the word to describe animals. If an animal is new and unfamiliar to us, we refer to it as a "strange creature." In our science fiction, creatures from other planets may be rational and willful, but they are called *creatures* to stress their difference from us. As creatures they frighten us and have something uncanny and unknown about them.

In our literature and daily lives we seldom refer to ourselves as creatures; the word is reserved for beings among which we feel we do not belong. We are different from them. Man thinks of himself more as a creator than as a creature: he himself makes monsters and tries to train and subdue the other animals of the world for his purposes. It is man's business to understand and to make other things; he is a creator. It is even his business to make himself.

Yet as human know-how increases, and man's ability to do more and more, although his present becomes ever more conductive to luxury living his future grows dimmer and dimmer. As if political, economic, and social problems were not enough, man, as we well know, is presently on the way to making the earth unfit for human habitation. The creator who finds it difficult to think of himself as a creature does not seem to be a good creator. But a Creator who is the ultimate Source of reality must be good, for what could corrupt him?

That man's creativity is tainted is unmistakably shown by the polluted skies and societies within which he lives. Reactions to our present predicament are varied and interesting. Some people think all we need is more time; in their view, it would seem, the mere passage of time will bring a solution to man's problems. Others feel that time is making things worse; they lament its passage and look only to a return of "the good old days." They observe that human problems have increased and become more complex with the passage of the years; going back in time is consequently the way to return to simplicity. Still other persons suggest that science actually negates time in any sense that makes it personally significant. They point out that whenever we make what is called a scientific prediction about the future, it is made on the basis of what is known now; in such circumstances, we destroy any radical newness the future might have by extending our present to it.

Is it possible that man's creativity lacks one principal ingredient: the acknowledgment that it is created? What could such an acknowledgment mean? Certainly not that we or anyone else could describe the process by which man and the universe came into being in the first place. The Christian doctrine of creation is not a description in systematic terms of how God produced the reality we know. In the last chapter we noted that God can be said to creat *ex nihilo*—out of nothing—only because he stands outside of all system. As personal presence he is beyond the type of reality we can describe as an object or with which our minds can form a totality.

But if the "how" of God's creation is not known, that the universe *is* created and that man *is* a creature can still have significance for us. We do not have to know how something is done to know that it is done. Even so, the fact that man is a creature must make some difference to us now; it cannot be just a statement about the past. What it means may be precisely what man's present creativity lacks. The essence of creation would have to be something men cannot give themselves; that is, it would have to be something they find and receive, which would, of course, explain why it can make them.

What fills these requirements?

Presence. A presence man cannot escape. Such presence will have to be acknowledged even when we try to deny it, and that is precisely the type of Presence we have discovered God to be. Presence which is the Source of all meaning is Presence which cannot be escaped, even when a person meaningfully tries to argue against it. The act of creation is above all an act that does something. For any agent to act it must be present, and presence itself is active. Man becomes a person only by means of the presence of other people and the meaning for which they are responsible in the culture into which he is born; the presence of another person calls man to creativity; and we have just noted the fact that presence is the source of all meaning. Only a Presence different from ours can give meaning to, and so be the source of, the worldly structure through which all human presence expresses itself. The absolute difference we have discovered in personal presence—that difference which enables personal confrontation to take place and which cannot be captured in any system or totality—makes presence the only adequate source of such a system as we discover the universe to be.

Let me repeat once more: although we do not know the "how" of creation, that we *are* creatures is still a meaningful statement. To know the "how" of creation would be to know "God's system," but God is by definition the One who stands outside of system as the Absolutely Other. As ultimate Presence he is the Source of all expression and all system; that is why he is different from us. God is present in human presence, and he is present in all meaning as its ultimate guarantee, but he completely transcends man in his Presence. God transcends man's faculties not only individually but collectively. He is uncontrollable. He is independent. To know him experientially as Presence *is* to know that we do not know him essentially for what he is in a way that would relativize him or enable us to think of him adequately in our terms. Our terms and our concepts are precisely what our experience of him as Presence shows him to be absolutely different from. He expresses himself differently from us. He does not say what we say, for he speaks the conditions of what we say; our speaking begins by using his speaking. He enables us to speak and to create by freely giving us the conditions of the only speech and creativity we know—our life in the world through our bodies. Our experience of him guarantees both his mystery and our creaturehood.

As a result of what has been said so far it may be seen that creation is not an isolated fact, separated from man, which he discovers as an intellectual curiosity. It is instead a meaningful relationship between persons, and it can be nothing less. A "lower" explanation of creation than personal presence would be no *explanation* at all.

God unifies all men by the presence of his difference to them. Man's complete being stands before God's presence and is called by that presence. Because he is different from us, all our being is located before God; which means that God's presence to us gives us our location in reality. To be located by God's presence is to be created. By locating us through his presence God makes us belong *here*. God makes us feel at home in our kind of being. To be able to accept with gratitude the kind of being he is, is the special gift of mother love to a child; a child's feeling of belonging and security can be received only from another, and the presence or absence of the love that makes such feeling possible plays an important role in the development of a person, as we shall see in the next chapter. But our feeling of belonging where we are because of the presence of God to us does not mean that God confines us where we are for the future. I am located here and can accept my being where it is because of God's presence; but as so located by his presence my whole being is a reference beyond itself to him. His presence, therefore, constantly calls me beyond myself and my present location into his love and into his world.

Because God's presence to man enables man to accept and find his whole self where he is, man finds his complete being related to God. Such a relationship to God's presence is more basic than thought, as I have suggested earlier, for it is a relationship which calls thought into action and gives thought the significance it has. The basic orientation of our whole being toward God in a manner that is prior to thought —the basic intentionality of our being toward God—is the essence of "being created." "Being created" makes sense in that the meaningfulness of man depends upon it, but that very fact means that man cannot master or fully understand by any of his faculties the relation of creaturehood that constitutes him.

If we have seen that "being created" means living in the presence of God, we have seen that "creation" is not first an idea we have in our minds and subsequently go out to look for in experience. Creation, the presence of God to us, is a relation so basic to man's experience that it defines that experience. It enables our experience to be itself. God's presence *calls* for man's development, and so is the context of all his behavior, actions, and projects.

Before turning to a discussion of the ultimate difficulty of the Christian doctrine of creation, let me call attention to one advantage of understanding the doctrine as so far presented. Other people have sought for an experiential doctrine of creation in the history of Christianity, and I have earlier mentioned Friedrich Schleiermacher's definition of creation as the feeling of absolute dependence upon God. Schleiermacher himself, as duly noted, did not equate feeling with our passing emotions, and it is most important that that identification *not* be made by anyone who is trying to make his religion experientially significant. If the doctrine of creation is true at any one moment it is true at every moment, which means that if *it* is going to be recognized at a feeling level it must be something that can be constantly felt.

Experience suggests that there are many times in our lives when we do not feel dependent. At those times we may intellectually acknowledge that we are not completely self-sufficient in the world, but as far as the way we live is concerned that acknowledgment is a gratuitous abstraction. It has no motivational value at all. Creatures, in fact, do have a type of independence; if they did not, there could be no atheists!

Full and content after a satisfying meal, all I want to do is lie down and rest, comfortable in my enjoyment. Dependence upon God may be something I acknowledge intellectually at the time, but it is completely external to my feelings. Feelings of dependence are lost to feelings of satiety. I want nothing but sleep, and I expect to wake up "hungry for the kill"—energetic and active. To try to talk about feelings of dependence which are supposed to occur within my feelings of independent satisfaction is an attempt to detract from my sensuous enjoyment of life. And to tell me that I should not have the individual enjoyment I have is to attack my identity as a singular person. Anyone should rebel against such an attack, and at the feeling level everyone does, even the most religious person. Sensuous enjoyment in itself is good precisely because it is a source of my singular identity as a person.

"Presence," however, detracts from nothing that is mine. I and every aspect of my being are able to be themselves in it. The presence of God bestows status upon us, but the status it gives us is one which refers beyond itself to another. "Being that refers itself to another" is a good definition of a creature.

"Creation" as "presence" does not try to prove its point by negation; it does not try to detract from or deny in any way the reality we are. Such presence actually posits us for the kind of being we are; it gives and fulfills our being in two senses. Such presence of God calls us to be more than we have been in the past and are in the present. It is a constant call to newness and adventure, and so may be said to offer us new being. Secondly, the presence of God calls us to be fully responsible for ourselves. Such responsibility, the highest perfection of freedom and personal maturity, can only be accomplished in the presence of another. A person is his fully creative self only as he is accountable for himself in the presence of another. To be completely accountable to another person, as we are to God, is to be completely dependent, but in a way that encourages—to the point of constituting—our free, autonomous action. We can be accountable only for what we freely do; accountability therefore encourages freedom. Being called by the presence of God to be, in a responsible way, more than we are is to experience positively the "dependent independence" that defines the nature of a creature.

Creaturehood so experienced can be described in words that have meaning for reason, but the relationship of creaturehood itself transcends our thought. In this way reason and feeling can reinforce each other by something which is beyond each and can be recognized by each. Thus man is permeated in all his dimensions by recognition of the truth of creaturehood which is his being.

Our discussion of the greatest problem associated with the Christian doctrine of creation, as indicated, still awaits us. I mentioned the nature of this awkwardness some time ago in speaking of the scandal of creation as Christians understand it, but one must in no way minimize the difficulty of the Christian doctrine here by noting that it has already been referred to. It is a difficulty that offends not just our reason but our common sense; in fact, it is so opposed to social custom that it often seems repugnant to us. In many—perhaps most—cases it prevents the truly Christian doctrine from being intellectually investigated altogether. This repugnance also keeps many people who want Christian peace in their lives from discovering it. It withholds them from their Christian identity and so from truly Christian living.

The greatest difficulty with the Christian doctrine of creation is the difficulty of letting ourselves be loved! It is hard to be a creature because it is hard to accept being loved completely. It is hard to accept God as Creator, but that is the beginning of Christianity.

We all want to be loved—but just the right amount. The degree for which we feel the need, the degree for which we call, with which we feel comfortable. The point is, love can make us feel uncomfortable.

Nothing makes us feel more guilty than someone who does too much for us. That is the way literally to overcome us, to make us feel helpless. We never experience guilt so strongly as when someone obviously does more for us than we deserve. On certain social occasions such as testimonial dinners we may be extravagant in our praise of each other, but such hyperbole is accepted social practice. It is consented-to social hypocrisy, a favor we do each other on an exchange basis. Generally speaking, the experience of having someone sincerely do too much for us is not too frequent an occurrence in our lives, and it is a good thing. Spending our lives doing less than we should for others requires the protection of other people at least doing no more than they should for us.

When someone loves us too much, we have to question him instead of ourselves. In that way we are forced to be with another, breaking the internal dialogue we have with ourselves that excludes others. Someone's doing too much for me appears at first to be an act for which he alone is responsible, but in the end it highlights my own responsibility. I cannot avoid recognition of my responsibility in the situation, for although the person acts the way he does because of the way I appear to him, this is an appearance and an action which I responsibly do not want. In any thoroughgoing analysis, we always discover that we are ourselves only with another: in virtue, because it is another who calls us to creativity; in guilt, because it is always in the presence of another that we default and are noncreative.

To be a creature is to be given too much. It is to be given too much before we can say No, for creation is our beginning and we all know that we do not deserve to be. We just *happen* to be. We begin with an event, a gift, a giving. This is why Christianity, which begins with an event, a gift, a giving, can speak so immediately to us and to our needs. Both we and Christianity are historical, and neither we nor Christianity are ourselves unless we are making history. The Christian claim is that to make history in Christ's way is man's only true fulfillment.

Letting God love me is the mark of my being a creature. It is hard to let him love me completely; knowing myself guilty of so many hesitations, backslidings, withdrawals, and refusals, I know I am not worthy of complete love. Some love, yes; complete love, no. True love is defenseless, outgoing union with another, it is vunerability and exposure. In so frequently choosing defensive isolation, separation, and protection, we cannot allow ourselves a complete union with a God who is Love. It is hard for us to accept God as our Creator, for we must then accpt him as our lover; to do that, however, we must accept him as someone involved with our lives, not outside of them. Our awareness of our own guilt simply will not allow such an open relationship with him.

Secretly for me even to think that God loves me completely sounds like pride to our defensively tuned spiritual ears. There is no other way we can view the matter and be ourselves; our personal lives and our society allow no other view. We are, after all, proud enough with each other; there is no reason for being ridiculous with God. Actually, as I have tried to point out, to acknowledge God's complete love for me is not pride; it is my creation. It is to admit that I am created and that my creation is still going on.

If one is loved completely, there is nothing he can do but love others; he need prove nothing about himself in a defensive, hostile manner. Secured by such love, fear of death can be inverted into an even more sensitive fear of murder; fear for self can be converted into concern for others. Self-protection becomes transformed into the desire to enable others to become themselves. As we grow in the love God bestows upon us, we grow in our ability to see our Source outside ourselves; recognizing that we come from Another, we recognize that we become more ourselves by giving ourselves to others. We originate in the presence of Another in order to share that presence with others. To let God love one completely will not lead to selfish unconcern for others, for God's love *is* such concern and can only produce itself.

The Christian doctrine that God creates because he is love is a sound one. We "arise" from love. That means that love is the basis of our lives, which means in turn that Christian love cannot be an element of a person's life which is expected to overwhelm and control other elements on the same kind of footing it has. Love cannot be a part which becomes the whole, for then other parts always have an equal claim. It must be a prior whole manifesting itself through parts which are always less than and subordinate to it. Christian love is primordial; it is the beginning. Something that is "later" can never make itself "first," but that is what we try to do when we will not first let God love us and let our lives be *that love overflowing*. We must be found in order to find, created in order to create, loved in order to love. For a Christian, love cannot be obtained from a part of life. It is a basic disposition that flows through parts; it is a presence which, because it affects all our being, must be given to us.

Because love is an event and creation an event, we can know creation for what it is in Jesus Christ and the event of his love in our lives. Upon such an understanding it is obvious that creation is an event still going on, not the formal statement of something over and done. We participate in God's act of creation by living creatively with Jesus Christ in the presence of the Father. As indicated earlier, a person's redemption or recreation in Jesus Christ is the experiential key to his understanding of God's creation in general.

It has been suggested that to be loved by Christ, who is the Father's love for us, is to be created. Still another experiential key to the doctrine of creation is the experience of being found. If you have ever been lost or know somebody who has been lost, you know that being found is something someone else must do for you. In some circumstances we have no choice about letting another person find us. But because of our free will, in our conscious lives with God we must *let* him find us. In religion we are not found by saying we are found but by *being* found. The dependence we have on another person when he tells us what has gone on in a meeting at which we arrive late, and helps us find our place in a report from which someone is reading, is a matter-of-fact but significant illustration of the meaning of being found. To let another help us find our place in such a manner enables us to belong to the group with a fullness of meaning that would otherwise be impossible.

To say that we must let ourselves be found by God is simple enough; the question is, how do we do it? We do it by letting the Father *locate* us here. The known, open acceptance of being where we are is fundamental to the practice of Christianity and results from properly understanding the doctrine of creation. Acceptance of oneself for what he is, where he is, shows that Christianity is based on reality and confronts it, rather than offering people a means by which they can flee reality. The doctrine of creation teaches us to accept the fact that we are *here*, but here as filled by God's love. Being so located, we become creative where we are, for the Father's love is always so much more than we are that it overflows us and pushes us beyond ourselves. Lack of being loved leads to feeling constantly empty—an explanation of the attempt of many people to get as much as they can from others under the name of business competition. A hungry ego needs constant feeding.

My faith is vain if I do not believe that God loves *me*. Love is always personal and penetrating. To allow myself to be found by God is the only way I can experience God's love for me, which love in turn *is* my identity. For the Christian to think otherwise is self-hatred. Acknowledged masters of Christian living throughout the centuries have consistently emphasized in their lives and writings the primacy of God's love for them. Contemporary readers of their works, for reasons which we have previously seen, frequently find their assertions scandalous. Julian of Norwich, a fourteenth-century woman, and Nicholas of Cusa, a fifteenth-century man, are two good examples. Julian wrote: "It is God's will that I see myself as much bound to him in love, as if all that he hath done he had done for me. And thus should every soul think in regard of his Lover."[1]

Nicholas, when asked by a community of men to help lead them into the mysteries of the Christian life, used as a teaching instrument an icon of God whose painted eyes seemed to be looking directly at a person no matter where he stood before the picture. There are numerous pictures of this type today, some of animals, some of human beings. Asking the monks to look at the picture from different positions, Nicholas taught that in the Presence of God, as in the presence of the picture, each person is looked at as if no one else were being observed at all. He says that God, who is Absolute Being, is as completely present to all as if he cared for no one else.[2]

It is not pride for Christians to think that Jesus died for *them*, for he did die for them—and for all men, but for each man in a way which shows that God loves him for the singular person he is. To accept the fact that every person in the world is specifically created by the love of God—a fact proved by the presence of God to every person in the world —is to understand how, in the Christian sense, individual persons are above universal principles and general categories. For a Christian every person is a whole in himself, worthy of infinite respect in his personal presence; no person is a mere example of a universal principle that is more than he. That truth is shared by Søren Kierkegaard, the famous Protestant theologian in the nineteenth century, and by Karl Rahner, the well-known Roman Catholic theologian of the twentieth century.

In his study of the dread Abraham experienced, when in faith he offered to sacrifice his only son, Isaac, to God, Kierkegaard concluded that it is the paradox of faith that the particular is higher than the universal.[3] He contended that each person stands in an absolute relation to the Absolute which is above universal laws and principles. Individuals without faith are less than the universal, and so, for example, are bound by the laws of ethics. The prohibition of murder is such a law. But God seeks to relate to every person in a more intimate way than by law. So it was that God spoke to Abraham; Abraham's dread was not only the loss of his son, but the anguish and horror of wondering whether or not he was a murderer.

Kierkegaard's analysis of the biblical story of Abraham offering to sacrifice Isaac was not intended to justify the wholesale breaking of ethical laws in the name of faith; it was intended to show that God does not create and rule his people in a mechanical way. Each person has a special, irreplaceable relation to God which lifts him out of the crowd. In that respect Karl Rahner writes:

One day the completed kingdom of God will come. Then there will be only individuals each with his own face and his own destiny which God's purely personal love has given to each one. And these unique beings will be eternal because they were always more than just examples of the universal. But these individuals are loving individuals. And love is both unique and all-embracing. And so these unique beings form the communion of saints, the eternal kingdom of the love of God who is both One and All. And in it he is in everyone because he embraces all. For love unites by the very fact that it sets free and differentiates.[4]

God's love for me is my location in reality if I acknowledge God as Creator. The doctrine of creation means that we find ourselves loved before we can try to be lovable; it means that there is a reason for self-respect even before we can try to make ourselves respected. Being loved by God—our creation —is the basis for the love of self which precedes loving others. True love of self is possible only if we first accept God's love of us and love ourselves in his way; that is why love of self is not selfishness. That is why we can be told to love others as we love ourselves.

We hear much about "identity crises" these days. "Who am I?" is one of our favorite questions. As the term has entered the mainstream of our lives and conversation, however, it is frequently misunderstood. An identity crisis is a crisis of *growth*. It is a crisis of change, not a state to luxuriate in or a means of escaping from reality into one's problems. An identity crisis is not solved simply by being able to identify one's state or one's nature now. The question, "Who am I?" really is a question about the future. It means, "What am I to become?"

The point is clear enough to Erik H. Erikson, the psychologist responsible for the term's popularity. He writes that the word crisis "no longer connotes impending catastrophe, which at one time seemed to be an obstacle to the understanding of the term. It is now being accepted as designating a necessary turning point, a crucial moment, when development must move one way or another, marshalling resources of growth, recovery, and further differentiation. This proves applicable to many situations: a crisis in individual development or in the emergence of a new elite, in the therapy of an individual or in the tensions of rapid historical change."[5]

Erikson is a developmental psychologist who has emphasized the identity crisis of youth; a good deal of additional work has concerned itself with the crisis of old age. The crisis of the middle-aged female has long been studied, and now attention is being turned toward the middle-aged male. He too, it turns out, has a crisis, and although it has long been overlooked it is no less real for the omission. The male middle-age crisis seems to begin about the late thirties and is frequently accompanied by a notable personality change. About that time in a man's life he may begin a considerable amount of stock-taking about himself: he questions the meaning of his life up to then and begins to ask himself with a new seriousness and a new perspective what he expects to get out of life before he dies. He realizes that the type of life he is presently living is most likely the one he will live until he dies, with the possible exception of some years of retirement in which he does not know what he will do. He feels trapped in his job, trapped by his debts, trapped by the expectations of society, and trapped by his wife and children. Middle-aged men have high rates of suicide, coronary attack, depression, and alcoholism.

Every person needs self-esteem, and such esteem is impossible to sustain in one's life unless it is nourished by at least some personal success. We need to succeed in some type of activity in order to be ourselves, a subject about which I shall have more to say in the next chapter. But the middle-aged man frequently finds that what he once thought was success has actually turned out to be a type of failure. His apparent success in business has resulted only in increased competition and threats from those who covet the outward signs of success he now enjoys. In his feeling of being trapped by his job and family, the venture that leads to repair of his sense of accomplishment and self-esteem in a number of instances turns out to be an affair with a younger woman. A considerable amount of literature has recently appeared in which such extramarital affairs are said to be only harmless outlets for the suffering male. With the substitution of a few words, major areas of the female middle-aged identity crisis can be described in just about the same way as the male. Women feel trapped as well as men.

The harmlessness of such extramarital affairs is the issue to be decided rather than the label to be applied to a social phenomenon, no matter how widespread it may be. Physical intimacy is not the same as personal intimacy, and the former cannot simply substitute for the latter. Physical intimacy is meant to be a means to, and expression of, personal intimacy. The highest personal intimacy can be attained only with people who have shared our history with us. Because we are temporal in our being, we need people who have known us a long time in order to be ourselves. On a full understanding of the person, temporal intimacy is a factor in sexual intimacy for which the presence of a young body can in itself never compensate.

The fundamental issue must be "What is a person?" Only after that has been decided can we know what true self-esteem in about. Descriptions of behavior and correlations of their occurrence in an "average lifetime" tell us nothing about what a person is meant to be. The fidelity and responsibility necessary to remain true to one's promises are a form of creativity less often discussed in popular articles than sexual promiscuity. The questions of the basic meaning of human life, how meaning itself is possible, and the possibility of living one's life in the intimate presence of God—all the issues with which religion is concerned—have been dismissed as irrelevant if one is able to call anything "harmless" without considering them. But the religious contention is that nothing is meaningless in life; everything is significant. If one activity has less meaning than another, the activity with less meaning is harmful to full personal development if it is substituted for an activity with more meaning.

If a person does not realize the profound sense in which he *is* the body he lives, he will tend to minimize the personal significance of the activities he carries on through his body. And because the body we live is the means by which we live in and know the world, a person's whole relation to the world will be affected by that viewpoint. When both the body and the world have less than fully personal meaning, our bodies and the world tend to become external and foreign to us. Seeing no personal identity immediately in them, either we misuse them and so find ourselves in the drug and ecological emergencies facing us today, or they become so strange to us that we no longer feel at home in them. In that case we have become schizophrenic, the most widespread psychological malady of our day.

There is a sense in which a Christian constantly lives in an identity crisis, for he must constantly ask himself, "What does God want me to become? What does God want me to do?" There is no alternative to growth for man, because God always calls him from beyond himself into the future. The Christian vocation is to take change, which constantly occurs in the world, and transform it in Christ into growth. The Christian doctrine of creation means that a person always has enough stability and security to dare to try to change the world for the better.

I have said that we must let God find us here—locate us *here* in his creative love. But this is not to say that *here, this,* is what God has created us for. God's creation goes on because he is constantly present with us. Creation is not finished, and God is not finished with us. We are located *here* only so that we can go *there;* we can have a change of place only if we begin in a place, and a place beyond where I am now is always God's goal for me. God's goal for all men is their everlasting growth in his love. Because God is love he always does *more,* even in his own life. That is the insight conveyed by the doctrine of the Trinity.

To say that God is a Trinity is to say that in his own life he somehow begets and bestows. The Father begets a Son and bestows the Spirit. That is why it is not impossible for the Father to recreate his own creation: he gives, and then he gives to his own giving.

To such a life there is no end, and the Father offers to share that life with us. That is what it means to be a creature!

Notes

1. Julian of Norwich, *The Revelations of Divine Love*, trans. James Walsh, S.J. (New York: Harper & Brothers, 1961), p. 175.

2. Cf., Nicholas of Cusa, *The Vision of God* (New York: Frederick Ungar Publishing Co., 1960), preface and chap. 4.

3. Søren Kierkegaard, *Fear and Trembling, passim.*

4. Karl Rahner, S.J., *Nature and Grace: Dilemmas in the Modern Church*, trans. Dinah Wharton (New York: Sheed & Ward, 1964), p. 37.

5. Erik H. Erikson, *Identity: Youth and Crisis* (New York: W. W. Norton & Co., 1968), p. 16.

.4.

Time and the Problems of Man

In our day many can see the need, but fewer the basis, for courage and hope in their lives. No one denies that courage is needed for healthy living; the problem is, where can it be found? Apart from the cataclysmic events of our times—war, poverty, racial injustice, pollution, drug abuse, political deception, and administrative corruption—we need courage to be ourselves in the simple unfolding of time. It takes courage to march rather than be carried into the future. But people may well ask, "Upon what can we ground the courage we so desperately need?"

Trust is the answer. It supplies the only basis for courage which is neither foolhardy nor presumptious. We now hear a good deal about the theology of hope, and much of that theological emphasis is helpful and of substantial Christian importance. The underscoring of Christianity's futuristic, eschatological orientation is vital, but the explication of Christianity in terms of hope has too frequently lost the dimension of presence we have been stressing. An understanding of the relation of trust to hope can remedy that defect, and it is a remedy I shall suggest in the course of this chapter. But before we consider their specific relation to each other, it will be helpful to examine the more general roles played by trust and hope in our lives.

Have you ever known a really free person? It is easy to envy him, to envy the completeness with which he lives. He has a mobility which makes him a pleasure to know and to be with. He can do different things with enjoyment; he is not afraid to expose himself to something new. He does not hide behind himself, pretending to be what he is not. His life is what it appears to be, that selfless involvement and interest in the world which are the perfection of the self.

The person who is truly free, although he always finds himself in particular circumstances, is never completely bound by those circumstances. Sickness, for example, does not spoil his zest for life, nor does disappointment rob him of his humor. Events which would force a weak person to be defensive are calmly accepted by the free man as new means of personal expression. If one really wants to dance, he can dance in an old suit as well as a new one. Aware as he is that worldly failure is an ever-present possibility in our human condition, the mere presence of this possibility does not deter him from undertaking new ventures. Some people are so overwhelmed by the possibility of failure that they are afraid to express their desires and inclinations. If someone has said a foreign language is hard, they are afraid to study it; if someone has asked them to make a speech at a large meeting, even though they have good ideas they are afraid to try to express themselves before others. There are people who so anticipate the possible troubles that may occur on a trip that their vacations are ruined.

The blessing of trust is freedom to be oneself. Trust is the backbone of personal affirmation; it liberates a person so that he can use his liberty. Trust enables our first answer to life to be Yes. If we trust in God we will never be asked "Why did you hesitate?" as Peter was asked by Christ in the story of his walking on the water, when Peter began to sink.[1] Trust in God gives us a deep reason for daring to move ahead in life, but it is not the kind of deep reason we can find by withdrawing from reality into ourselves. When we trust we live with God, thus we do not get bogged down in the infinite layers of self-reflection.

Trust enables one to want to do what he is doing, for it enables him to be himself while doing it. We have no idea how many people are hollow in their activities, inwardly withdrawing from the confident exterior they try to project. But a life that is all-pretending is a hard one, sapping our true creative energy. We cannot always be on a stage, performing. If we feel we must, we will never be able to catch up to the roles we play: in order to keep up our public appearance we will find ourselves increasingly committed to obligations we inwardly feel are too big for us. In these circumstances, we have to look for false ways to grow or artificial helps to relaxation.

Capacity to trust is one of the first aspects of ourselves we reveal in the world. How could it be otherwise? For trust is a natural correlate of dependence. In our early years we must trust others. To the extent that our trust is betrayed at that time, we find it increasingly difficult to develop into the free, full persons we should become. Let us listen to a psychiatrist on the subject.

Before the child develops any thinking or verbal expression of his emotions he learns to trust, since he experiences without consciousness that his needs for survival, growth, and development fit into his parents' needs to give gratification and protection in mutually adaptive, tender co-operation. This trust, this confidence, which precedes all rational thought processes, seems . . . to be the matrix or an early manifestation of religious experience. It grows with the growing individual and transcends the boundaries of the early environment; it embraces the universe of the broadening personality. This propensity to trust exists even when the parents are not trustworthy. In that case trust is driven underground, hiding behind defenses; but the propensity to trust cannot be abolished in any human being.

When the tender co-operation between parents and child fails, the danger signal of anxiety appears. . . . Every step forward into undiscovered territory is loaded with danger and anxiety. For instance, the child makes his first daring attempts to learn to walk; hesitantly he leaves the protective and supportive arms of his mother; he stumbles, bumps his head, seeks protection again in his mother's arms; and cries as if he would never try again. . . .

An atmosphere of excessive anxieties interferes with the development of natural trust. The trusting child is needy, but not greedy; he learns to wait, and to conform; he shows great adaptability to what the parents can or cannot offer him. The greedy child is haunted by excessive anxieties; his protesting rage estranges him further from parents who are unable to meet his needs. The child that cannot trust barricades himself behind self-centered defenses of despair, defiance or sullen detachment.[2]

Dr. Edith Weigert, just quoted, also points out that anxiety comes from the Latin word *angustus,* which means narrow. The anxious individual is one who is hemmed in, unable to express himself in the world. His behavior centers upon himself in a closed way instead of manifesting and increasing his openness to the world. Loneliness, self-protection, and self-justification become his ever-increasing portion because of his inability to trust others and expose himself to them. Self-centeredness becomes his lot, and in this case the lot buries him! Loneliness leads to helplessness, for the morbid need to isolate oneself from others cuts one off from their possible strengthening influence.

Cut off from the growth and development that normal trust allows, a person repeats in all his later interpersonal relations the original conflicts that arrested his development.[3] What should be new and exciting experiences for him become only new settings within which he surreptitiously relives the event that defeated him. No matter what new material life furnishes him, he always structures it with the same protective tactics he used in his first defeat. Lacking the sympathy and acceptance that grow out of trust, such a person is often driven to seek despotic power or hoped-for release in sexual exploitation. Lacking the confidence trust engenders, he finds himself incapable of expanding the horizons of his life in a normal way.

Substitutions for the original need for trust, such as domination and lust, are never successful. It is because selfish impulses cannot replace man's primary need to trust others and be trusted by them that the attempted substitutions are insatiable and compulsive in character. They never leave a person alone, for they can never really satisfy. The need for trust is so genuine in man that the presence of its counterfeit allows him no peace.

It is a commonly recognized fact that man is subject to anxiety and fear because he lives in time. Freedom, too, feeds on time, for if there were not the absence which is futurity freedom would have no room in which to act. Freedom cannot operate where everything simply is; it needs alternatives and possibilities if it is to have anything to choose.

What do people fear? What are they anxious about? The future. The unforeseen, the unexpected, old age, examinations—in doctor's office or in school; accidents, change, sickness, or death strike terror in the hearts of many because they are specters of the future.

Beset by such worries an anxious person frequently tries to escape time (or at least noticing time) by the way he lives in the present. Such a person becomes compulsive. He tries to lose or bury himself so completely in what he is doing in the present that he will escape noticing the uncertainty of the future. The present, however, can never completely protect one from the future because it is constantly open to the future; its growing edge is toward the future. Consequently many people, in their desperate search for security, are driven to try to live in the past. Since everything in the past is already over, there are no longer any open possibilities in it. Thus the past cannot threaten us with new challenges. Some persons are so weak that they can find their religious security only in the past; they try to equate Christianity with simple acceptance of some previous theological system, in an attempt to escape the challenge that theological uncertainty would hurl at them in the present.

But none of these devices works; to be a human person, we have seen, is to *be* a past, present, and future. I cannot pick one dimension of time and try to live exclusively within it. I cannot, for example, be my true and whole self if I try to live only in the past. It would be as if I tried to crawl inside myself and live only in my spleen. We are not dimensionless points in space and time; we are spatial and temporal extensions even in the most intimate core of our personal being.

Commitment to something in the unforeseen future *is* me. My very being forces me to trust. Even if I spend my life sitting in my chair in my room, the simple process of growing older moves me constantly into the future and calls on me to trust. No matter how old we are, if we exist, we journey forward. The future without trust is fear and bondage, but with trust it is freedom and adventure. "Time's tyranny," the inexorable movement so many people dread, can be humanized if we understand the real purpose of time. For *time is the agent God uses to draw out our trust; the purpose of time is to allow man to trust in God.* For the Christian, time is trust.

Leaving our consideration of trust for a moment and turning our attention toward hope, we should notice Jürgen Moltmann's remark that "from first to last, and not merely in the epilogue, Christianity is eschatology, is hope, forward looking and forward moving, and therefore also revolutionizing and transforming the present."⁴ The eschatological and temporal emphasis of such a view recalls us to basic biblical themes and also incorporates many of the most penetrating insights of contemporary thought about man's nature. Because of Christianity's fundamental orientation toward the future, theological concepts may be said not to fix reality in any permanent way; the only function of such concepts is to anticipate the future and to illuminate the present with hope for the new future God has promised us in Jesus Christ. Immutability and the *status quo* are the worst enemies of the God of the Bible. The Greek notion of God's revelation as the placing of the eternal in time leads to an "epiphany religion" quite different in nature from the biblically oriented religion of promise, in which God somehow enters history instead of negating it. In the biblical witness, God promised his people a Messiah and a Kingdom; the revelation of God in Jesus is the fulfillment of those promises.

In a religion of promise history is important; it is the *means* of God's revelation instead of a medium foreign to it within which timeless truths are revealed. Because of the temporal nature of revelation, transformation—not interpretation—is the purpose of theology. The Christian life is one of historical openness, not one of conceptual clarity, for God's revelation always exceeds our expectation; the future is more than the present or the past, and even Christ ascended to an unknown glory which lay ahead of him after his resurrection. These themes indicate that Christianity can only be lived in the world of time, and they turn history into mission. God's revelation to man in Jesus is historical, and no man can live the history Jesus inaugurates without participating in Jesus' mission. To live with Jesus is to make history the vehicle of God's purpose and promise.

If Christianity is "from first to last" hope, we may wonder what role hope plays in our lives from the point of view of descriptive psychology. We have already seen the importance of trust from such a viewpoint.

In the psychological perspective, hope is associated with action; it is a prerequisite for action because it is an expectation of goal attainment.[5] Hope is an important factor in the security felt by beings who live in time, for it is the positive expectation of future goal achievement. It is, in other words, the feeling of a high probability of future success in one's undertakings.

The more successful a person has been in achieving his goals in the past the more likely he is to attempt to achieve his goals in the future. Even if he experiences a failure, the greater the number of successes he has had in the past, the more likely he is to continue his performance. Partial success in the past seems to lead to more persistence and ingenuity in the present than either previous total success or total failure. This is reasonable enough, for a record of partial success and partial failure shows a person that reality is not inevitably cast for or against him; he always has a chance. Ethnic and minority groups who have been so long "kept in their place" that they have no remembered past of goal attainment in political, economic, academic, and social life tend to withdraw from such involvement altogether. Repeated failure and the absence of achievement have taught them hopelessness, and so they do not attempt significant goal achievement in those areas. At best they substitute lower goals which do seem possible of attainment for higher ones. In this light it is understandable why achievements in sports and entertainment instead of law and medicine are the primary hope of deliverance for modern ghetto people. A big car and flashy clothes are marks of achievement that are obvious and objective; they are something it is possible to hope for. We can also understand why black history, for example, is so important for black people of today; their lived memory gives them little basis for hope, but if they can identify with a racial past which preceded their exploitation in slavery there is much they can be proud of and upon which they can hopefully face the future. The same is true of the American Indian. Interestingly enough, the discovery of identity and hope on the part of red and black men in the United States frequently causes the white man to have an identity crisis of his own as his previous security is threatened. The confrontation of crises in identity with crises in security is a basic way of describing the social and political turmoil a major portion of the world is experiencing today.

The adoption of a subgoal easier to achieve than an ultimate goal is a way frequently chosen to avoid anxiety. Parents whose children had leukemia have reported that adopting short-range goals that could be fulfilled, such as taking their children to a movie, was what sustained them during the final phases of their children's illness.[6] Inversely, a person who is apathetic may advance to a state of anxiety as a result of an increase of hopefulness. It was noted, for example, that airmen in World War II who had been fatalistic or at least bitterly resigned to death sometimes developed great anxieties during their last missions, when they began to have a realistic hope of survival. E. L. Quarantelli is cited as stating that "persons in panic feel powerless to bring the threat itself under control but they do not despair of getting out of danger by fleeing." "He reports [the writer goes on to say] that if the person feels that he cannot possibly escape, he does not panic, does not flee, but sits down, so to speak, to await death."[7]

In any event, the role of past success should not be underestimated in its influence on a person's hopefulness for the future. It has been observed in a given factory that fifty-three men who had been promoted decreased their visits to the infirmary, while thirty-two men whose occupational status had decreased increased their infirmary visits. Assuming that physical ailments or concerns are manifestations of anxiety, the study suggests that an anticipated probability of low goal attainment increases anxiety.[8]

The importance of the past in the face of the future even

shows in certain experiments that have been performed with
rats. At the University of Minnesota it was discovered that
dewhiskering laboratory rats in no way affected their ability
to swim; they would swim for over fifty hours before giving
up. When wild rats were dewhiskered, however, it was found
that 10 per cent of them died before being placed in water,
while the other 90 per cent died within two minutes of entering the water. If the dewhiskered wild rats were placed in
water several times but rescued before they could drown,
they too swam for over fifty hours. It would seem that they
were "taught hope" by being rescued.[9]

Besides the experience of success and failure in one's own
past, the expectation of other people is a most important
factor in encouraging hope. Membership in a hopeful group
increases one's hopefulness, and it has been found that com-
bat fatigue is better treated when a soldier can retain his
group identity with his unit than when he is sent to the rear.
People contemplating suicide who communicate their needs
to others either verbally or by abortive attempts on their
lives, go on to suicide if they receive "a fearful reaction from
others, signifying little hope. . . . If they did not receive an
anxious, hopeless response from others, they were unlikely to
go on to suicide."[10]

Again, mothers and mother surrogates are associated with
goal attainment. Their presence lowers anxiety, and there
even seems to be some evidence that first children and only
children have their anxiety lowered more by the presence of
another person than do subsequent children, perhaps due to
the fact that the initial experience of the later children with
their parents is not so consistently supportive. A significant
factor in prisoners of war giving up hope has been found to
be the sight of other prisoners dying; we all know what the
sight of another person's illness does to a hypochondriac.

We began our discussion of the psychological description
of hope by noting its relation to action and the expectation

of goal attainment. The inability to act lessens hopefulness and arouses anxiety, for past successes have come through action. The corollary of that statement is that action of any sort tends to lessen anxiety, and that is precisely what the evidence seems to indicate. Even trivial actions invoke hopeful schemas of success. After a person fails or believes he fails in a task in which he persists, restlessness, small movements, and twitches frequently develop in his behavior. A person practicing a difficult piece on the piano behaves quite differently from the way he would in a formal recital, and a room full of students taking an examination offers a considerable variety of such expressive activity. Ezra Stotland suggests that this may help explain why people tend to eat when they are anxious: eating has reduced hunger successfully in the past. Eating is therefore associated with goal attainment and hopefulness.[11] Even in the lower animals it has been found that when subjected to painfully loud noises, animals that run about, wash their faces, hide, or have some other energy outlet have significantly fewer audiogenic seizures than animals which do not release their energy, and some have none.

We may conclude this brief excursus with a summary statement from Stotland: "Since action is a part of the schema of adequately adaptive behavior, the organism's perceiving that it is acting or moving in some way would tend to arouse a schema of hopefulness, thus reducing anxiety. . . . When the organism cannot act in even unconsequential ways, hopelessness and anxiety increase. It is, of course, needless to say that actions that are effective and do make a difference reduce anxiety even more."[12]

The time has now come to offer a suggestion about the relation of trust to hope. We have seen that much present-day theological discussion is deficient in this regard, and we cannot in fact get much help on the point from such psychological sources as we have just observed. These studies do not help us because of the general way in which anxiety is defined for their purposes; it is simply equated with "physiological arousal and subjectively negative affect."[13]

But to equate anxiety with any "subjectively negative affect" is too general an identification; there are different sources of subjectively felt negative affects, and those differences are commonly used to distinguish anxiety from fear. Anticipation in time is a common factor in both anxiety and fear, but anxiety is an uneasy anticipation of a future in which no specific object is identifiable, while fear is such an anticipation aroused by a specifically threatening object. We fear something definite, but we are anxious about the future "in general."

With that clarification in mind we can distinguish trust from hope, because trust is the experience that overcomes anxiety, while hope is our means of overcoming fear. We began this chapter with some thoughts about courage, so we may bring it into discussion here.

For the moment, let us look primarily at trust and courage. They are allied virtues: each is positive and each is affirmative and forward-looking. But trust explicitly calls attention to an element that is often overlooked in courage and hope: the element of personal presence. As we ordinarily use the words, "courage," for example, emphasizes oneself, while "trust" emphasizes one's relation to another. We say, "He trusts in his friend." The use of the preposition "in" with trust shows its reference to someone or something outside itself. Classical thought considered courage, on the other hand, to be an individual rather than a social virtue. It was said to be something a person can exercise when he is alone; trust obviously relates us to another.

Trust, then, is a way of living in the presence of another person; it is a way of living *with* another. In trust the presence of the other is experienced as a source of meaning and consistency which exceeds objective representation; thus trust in another gives us a general feeling of security and openness toward the future. A child trusts his mother in learning to walk, and a man who trusts God is not afraid to walk with the world into the future.

While trust is based on the recognition of another person's infinite presence as presence, hope needs a goal. We trust in a person, but we hope *for* something definite. It is only because God the Father has given certain promises to men that Christianity can be a religion of hope. In the Judeo-Christian tradition, we have seen, God has promised men a Messiah— a Savior, and a Kingdom—God's ultimate goal for creation. Both promises, Christians believe, have been fulfilled in Jesus Christ, but in a special way. First of all, in a way which shows that God is *present* with us in the world precisely as we are in the world—the witness for which is the life and death of Jesus in the same historical time in which we live; and in a way which shows that the Father has the power necessary to defeat any foe—the witness for which is Jesus' resurrection from the dead. But the promises have not been fulfilled in a way that gives us final clarity about what our lives will be like when God is all in all.

Christianity is a religion of hope; it is oriented inexorably toward the future, but it is able to be a religion of hope only because it is first a religion of trust. The infinite presence of God is what makes the future hopeful, and Christians must experience his presence before they can hope for his future! No man has a clear image of God's final goal for creation; thus Christian hope for that goal always depends upon a trust in God's presence which makes the hope possible. On the other hand, because the future is one thing rather than another (for the future is distinct and different from the present) we Christians must hope for something definite; we cannot just trust in God and withdraw from the world. In God's presence we must try to give his meaning to the world in the concreteness of the world, and receive his meaning in that same mode. Only through trust and hope, presence and expression, can we be our full selves. There is no personal religion without worldly expression, for to be a person is to be a presence in a world; any attempt to escape the world is an attempt to escape ourselves.

We cannot reduce religion to any one thing: hope, love, trust, humility, or faith. Reduction tends toward intellectualization and propositional expression. Religion is a presence, an event, not an idea; it is a life, not a proposition. That is why we must use symbols in our religious expression; symbols, like our lives, are inexhaustible concrete wholes. As a matter of fact, what frequently look to us like clear ideas in religion—hope, love, trust, humility—are really only symbols of our actual lived relationship with God.

Because God is the living Father in whom we trust and for whose Kingdom we hope, and because he is the Creator who has made us temporal, thereby necessarily orienting us toward the future, he is a God of change. If we believe in a God of change (as a Christian must), then we can be enthusiastic about change in the world. If we believe in a God who only *permits* change instead of positively willing it, change becomes a threat. Change, in the latter view, means "I might lose what I have," and consequently I fear it. The Christian God of change who calls us into the future intends all change to be a source of personal growth; in this view we embrace change and say, "I must constantly change to get what God gives, for the Father wants me to be *more* with him in the future than I am now." The future is growth in love and in love's expression.

To miss the Christian message and believe in a God who only permits change instead of requiring it, makes one wonder how much change God can allow. This is like wondering how much evil a good God can permit, and—implicitly if not explicitly—the fearful believer actually equates change with evil. His stance in the world is backward-looking, while the world itself always changes. The only benefit that can come from religion in these circumstances is the removal of the faithful from the world. The ultimate perversion of historical Christianity is to see change itself as the problem of man instead of as the means of redemption and the possibility of solving problems.

Christians see the future as adventure; they must *want* a future that is different from the present. Christianity requires that something be happening, for it is founded in what has happened, and it can be itself only as what happened then continues to happen now. If Christianity cannot happen now, it is a delusion and a lie; under no circumstances can it be a theory. What once happened was a promise for the future given in the power of the resurrection; the risen presence of Jesus is powerful.

I always want tomorrow to come, for my presence with God always wants new expression. The infinitude of presence makes the future possible and makes us want the future. Presence necessarily overflows the expression of the present. God's presence produces trust, and the future is our hope.

One is "beaten" by time when he feels boxed up in any one of its dimensions. I am weighed down, for example, when things I have to do in the present stand between me and the future, making it impossible for me to see my way through to it. The liberation offered us in Christianity is the gift of the future in the present through the presence of the glorified, risen Christ with us now. He is our future come to us; thus all who recognize Jesus as the Christ have the future in the present. *For a Christian the consolation of the present is the presence of the future in it.* That presence frees me in the present, but in such a way that I want to live in the present, not avoid it. The presence of the risen Christ brings the consolation of the future to me, but that consolation is too big for the present to contain; consequently, there is no alternative but for the presence of the future to move me, in the present, toward itself. The presence of Christ in our lives is a source of continual growth and activity; it makes satisfaction with a present that is not changed impossible. The presence of the future in the present means that we must go beyond the present. That is why the Christian life is constantly new and exciting.

The future is meant to be the friend of man because Jesus Christ has called us friends. The Christian future enables us to be where we are without shirking or shrinking because it is the future offered to us with the same historical fullness and concreteness that our present life has.

If we trust in the future because it comes from a Source outside of and different from us, we cannot make a fantasy of it along lines that transform it into an escape from reality. Instead, the future becomes a new power for the acceptance of present reality, because it is the presence of power to change that reality. From the point of view of time, the significance of Easter—the founding event of Christianity— is that *the future works within the present.*

For a Christian *it is the future that is certain and the present that is not.* This realization, at one time, focuses creativity where it can be exercised (in the present) and destroys all anxiety about the future which is nonproductive. Of course, we do not have clear details about what the future will be, but in Christ we are sure of God's victory in it. The future, then, is unseen but certain, while the present is seen but uncertain (for *now* is when I am called to be creative). The relation of the future to the present is motivating and moving, for the future's relation to the present is above all dynamic, tendential, and beckoning.

What about the past? The past is composed of the futures of previous nows. A man cannot be hopeful without a hopeful past; in order to learn new ways of living people must be given a hopeful past—a fact, as we have seen, which must never be forgotten when the social expectancy of underprivileged people is set by those in political power. People are not given a new future when a single bill is passed in Congress or one reform is enacted in a city council. A new future that is personally significant can be given to suppressed people only when they have been given a new past. Entrance into the Christian community, the church, gives a person a specific past from which he can draw hope by identifying him with the previous history of God's chosen people and with the unique fulfillment of his promises to those people in the life, death, resurrection, and ascension of Jesus Christ.

In summary we may say that to trust in God is to welcome anything that can happen to us in the world. That is what it means to be in the world but not of the world. The only way we can avoid spending all our time thinking about ourselves is to trust in someone other than ourselves. In this sense trust liberates the self by freeing us from ourselves; to protect ourselves is no longer our first need. We are constituted by our being in the presence of God; that is why the direction of a healthy life is toward God and toward others in God.

Life with Christ is constant advance and growth. As St. Paul put it, and Gregory of Nyssa reemphasized in the fourth century, in the liberating Spirit of the Lord we go "from glory to glory."[14] To trust God is to let him do what he will through me rather than my doing what I can for him. Trust is our letting God do his best in us. To rely on God is to reveal God; to trust in him is to refuse to hide him in our lives.

Because of the presence of God, no person is alone. The assurance of that fact is the basis of trust. Whatever we do in life and whatever happens to us in life, we are with God and are meant to relate ourselves to him. St. Paul put it this way: "None of us lives to himself, and none of us dies to himself. If we live, we live to the Lord, and if we die, we die to the Lord; so then, whether we live or whether we die, we are the Lord's."[15] In other words, regardless of the circumstances of the moment, we are the Lord's and must trust him.

But Paul, like the early Jews—and any sensible person—does not advocate a blind trust. We must put our trust where hope is possible. There must be a criterion for trust, and that criterion must, in the end, be based on a power that can make itself felt in external events. Internal growth is never found apart from some external power. God has shown us that he merits our trust by what he has done for us in Jesus Christ. As St. Paul continues: "For to this end Christ died and lived again, that he might be Lord both of the dead and of the living."[16]

God has already taken decisive action for us in the resurrection of his only-begotten Son from the dead. Jesus Christ is the reason Christians trust in God. A Lord without power is a lord in name only. As we are not hurt by names, neither are we saved by them. God in Christ has established his lordship by a mighty act: an act which he promises to share with us. In his First Epistle to the Thessalonians, St. Paul again makes this essential point: "For God has not destined us for wrath, but to obtain salvation through our Lord Jesus Christ, who died for us so that whether we wake or sleep we might live with him. Therefore encourage one another and build one another up, just as you are doing."[17]

It is because God has already shown his power in Christ that our trust in him can be so complete. St. Paul, writing to the Philippians, said that the only important thing in his life was "that I may know him [Christ] and the power of his resurrection. . . ."[18] St. Athanasius maintained that the power of the cross was convincingly shown in the way Christ's disciples despised death. Having known and studied under people who had suffered in the early persecutions of the church, Athanasius was speaking about people he knew when he wrote: "But now that the Saviour has raised his body, death is no longer terrible; for all who believe in Christ tread him [death] under as nought, and choose rather to die than to deny their faith in Christ."[19]

Once we place our trust in God, within our free commitment, we meet an assurance which is absolutely certain.
Something has been done for us in Christ, and as we acknowledge this gift within us we are loosed from worldly anxieties
and tensions. We are still concerned for the world, but we are
no longer anxious within the world.

Another translation of the passage from Romans 14:8, already quoted, makes the meaning of the Greek more explicit
and may help to explicate this point. "Whether therefore we
live or die, we belong to the Lord." (NEB) Use of the word
"belong" in this translation makes the possessive of the
Greek more obvious. We *belong* to the Lord. Belonging indicates a relation which in one sense is beyond our control. We
most frequently use the concept in reference to things—
where, for example, an act of purchase binds property to a
person. In the affairs of the world, the purchase of a thing can
be final and complete. An object can become its owner's once
and for all.

God in Christ does not override our freedom and force us
to become his property. He calls us to be his adopted sons and
heirs, friends in his Kingdom and at his table. But once we
do freely offer ourselves to him, we are received by him with
the assurance and completeness of having been bought. We
experience this assurance in the midst of our free association.
Since we are bought, not selling, we can relax. Our purchase
was "an act of faith" on God's part; it was his assurance of love
to us, not his forcing us to be saved against our wills. That we
belong to the Lord means that the initiative is God's—that
peace is ours.

We trust in God because he is God. His power and intention are certain because he has shown both in Christ. Born
of a human mother into a world of toil, disease, opposition,
and death, Jesus Christ started where we do. It is within the
world as we find it that we come to know the Father's concern and love for us. The Christian vocation is not to rebel

against reality by trying to explain why the world should not be as it is; Christians don't know why! They know God as a person only in Jesus, thus they have no basis for arguing that God as a person should have made things differently than he did. In Christ one can know only acceptance and victory. Christ's power in the world was not shown by arguing that things should not be as they are, but by changing and overcoming things as he found them. The Christian answer to old facts is new facts; his people are here to continue the Father's creation of the world in Christ, not to lament the world.

Notes

1. Matthew 14:31, NEB.

2. Edith Weigert, M.D., "The Psychoanalytic View of Human Personality," in *The Nature of Man*, ed. Simon Doniger (New York: Harper & Brothers, 1962), pp. 7 and 9.

3. Cf. *Ibid.*, p. 19.

4. Jürgen Moltmann, *Theology of Hope*, trans. James W. Leitch (New York: Harper & Row, 1967), p. 16.

5. Cf. Ezra Stotland, *The Psychology of Hope* (San Francisco: Jossey-Bass, 1969), p. 2.

6. Cf. *ibid.*, p. 36.

7. *Ibid.*, p. 21.

8. Cf. *ibid.*, p. 30.

9. An experiment of Dr. John Brantner, Associate Professor of Clinical Psychology in the Department of Psychiatry at the University of Minnesota, as reported by the Rev. Richard F. Grein. Stotland reports a similar experiment by C. E. Richter, *ibid.*, p. 20.

10. Stotland, *op. cit.*, p. 145.

11. Cf. *ibid.*, p. 121.

12. *Ibid.*, p. 88.

13. *Ibid.*, p. 9.

14. Cf. 2 Corinthians 3:17 f., AV

15. Romans 14:7 f.

16. Romans 14:9.

17. 1 Thessalonians 5:9–11.

18. Philippians 3:10.

19. *Christology of the Later Fathers,* ed. E. R. Hardy, Library of Christian Classics, Vol. III. (Philadelphia: Westminster Press, 1954): 81.

.5.

Body-Meaning

A few years ago an actress known as "The Body" got considerable publicity.

There have been, and are, a number of people in Hollywood whom that title would fit. Jayne Mansfield, who met a tragic death in an automobile accident, comes to mind as someone who worked hard at the image. Her body was her identity, nothing less than the key to her whole style of living.

Her body was to her not just a thing, an object, although that is the way it was displayed; it was her life, her constant project. As she lived her body, it organized her life; through it she spent herself. It organized her time: what she would do, how long she would do it, when she would do it. It organized her space: where she lived, where she went, where she wanted to be. Such a life of the body can be a totally consuming one, absorbing all that a person says, thinks, does, desires, hopes for.

In picking an actress for illustration, have we taken an extreme example, totally different from ourselves? I think not, and a good deal of contemporary research backs that answer up. We are all bodies, and if we would pay more attention to those bodies as we live them from the inside, instead of thinking of them only as we see them from the outside, we would know more about ourselves than we now do. I have written about this subject elsewhere and drawn certain theological conclusions from the analysis, but must draw attention to some features of that discussion here.[1]

In summary fashion we may say that our bodies are the first sources of structure in our lives. It is through our bodies that we are placed in the world, and we have already seen that they are the center of our experiential worlds. For us, the sun remains "out there." It is because we are bodies that we can understand and use prepositions in our thought; we have seen that our bodies cannot be just objects, for they are the *means* by which we know objects. Because we are bodies we *are* an outside and therefore necessarily a relation to others; it is only through the body that we can express ourselves to others. The experience of our bodies is also our first introduction to the nature and use of power in the world. When an infant first holds its head up, turns over, and begins to crawl, he is introduced to a way of making a difference in the world that culminates in interplanetary rocket travel and the use of atomic power.

The body each one of us immediately lives at this moment is not just an object seen from the outside; it is a personal project, a style of living, an assembly of activities. The body we live is, first of all, the way we are in the world; it is the means by which we enter the world. We are born when our bodies are delivered, and we die when they cease to function.

The style of living to which we are accustomed radiates from our bodies outward. Comfort and convenience are centered in our bodies, but comfort and convenience do not end there. They motivate our lives and fill our hours. Most of us would be surprised, if not chagrined, by how much of our lives is influenced by the foods we like to eat, the service we like to receive, the car we like to drive, the house we want to live in, the deference we want to receive in society.

The body we live is the means of our basic orientation to reality. Bodily defects, just like bodily abilities, are primary factors in organizing the worlds in which we immediately live. Children learn to organize their worlds through play, adults through engineering; both are activities and extensions of our bodies.

The way a person feels about his body is a key to the way he feels about the world. Hypochondriacs prove the point. To be afraid of what will happen to one's body is a way of living in the world; such a person fears the world. His fear of how the world may affect him through his body actually shows that the world is only an extension of his concern for his body.

To be ashamed of one's body or a part of it is a way of living in the world, too. The way we compensate for our bodies takes a lifetime—and makes a life-style. Pride about one's body fills a lifetime and makes a life-style also. Concern for money, taxes, profits, pledges, apportionments, representation, neighborhoods, assessments, war, poverty, sex, and food are all bodily concerns or extensions of them. Money, for example, is power, and the basic kind of power we know is that which we have over our bodies and through our bodies over the world.

One way or another, the body we actually live is a project which defines our style of living and the kind of person we are. The body in the sense in which it is a project—that is, in the sense in which it is lived—is man as a person.

Man's life is a project and his body is a project; he knows neither project without the other. If we look at the roots of the word, "project" should be written pro-ject; the word literally means "to throw forward." Man's body, the first structure of his life, is, as project, future-oriented; it is active. For man, a project is promise, hope, creation. Man as a lived body in the world is thus a project; he is orientated toward the future, hope, and promise. He is the "not yet" always trying to become more.

Only dead bodies are static, and actually they are not static for they decay. No human body is static. It is the ultimate perversion of human nature to use the body as a reason for maintaining the *status quo,* for fighting change or trying to live in the past. Even if we use the body to fight change, our body ages and so changes us.

Every project we undertake, when we analyze its basic ingredients, is a way of organizing space and time. Space and time can be organized in different ways, however. There are people who live tidy lives and others who live less restrictively; there are people who are punctual and those who are never on time; people whose search for more money organizes everything they do; people who do not care about external appearance; people whom we say are "expansive" and aggressive; people who are retiring and diffident. As we organize our lives differently we develop different styles of living; thus as we actually live our bodies, pro-jecting ourselves through them, our bodies themselves become styles of living.

The body as an object is a place to hang stylish clothes, but as we live it, it is itself a style, a project. Since the body we live *is* space, simply by living it we are organizing space. As a project it also takes time; thus our lived body is a way we organize time. The space and time we organize by living our bodies is one with the space and time in which we experience the universe in its totality; which means that the styles of living which are our lived bodies are actually potential styles of organizing the universe. Our bodies as we live them are not objects; they are activities we try to extend further and further into the universe through our daily living and our scientific activity. Man seems potentially capable of having nothing less than a universal body!

Because the body locates us in the world, we belong to the world and can never be just spectators of it. If someone pushes us off a building we cannot be mere spectators of the fall. The fact that we *are* bodies makes us responsible for the world, for by being bodies we are constantly organizing a spatial and temporal structure which extends to other people and other things. We make one kind of world rather than another by trying to flee people as well as trying to be with them. Avoiding other people is a way of saying something to them just as much as asking them over for dinner. Because we are bodies we are always related to other people and are always saying something to them.

Man's being as a person is a polarity of presence and structure, and the body is the first principle of his structure. The body we live is not something to which we must give meaning before it is significant to us; it is meaningful to us in the first instance, and becomes a source of the meaning of other things because it is the primary location of our presence. The body gives location to presence, and to be a person is to be locatable. The body is thus a source of human responsibility, for to be responsible a person must "take a stand," "stand for something," defend one *position* rather than another.

The body is meaning for man because it is human presence as located. But in all that has been said so far about the body and its importance in human life—even in saying that man *is* his body—we have not denied that personal presence transcends the body. Personal presence is more than the body, but we are able to know it to be more only through the body and never without a body. Human presence needs the body in order to be itself, for body-meaning anchors us in the world.

Man as a person always has the bodily and communal aspects just mentioned, but these do not exhaust his nature. He is also linguistic. It is not that man is a being who uses words merely as something outside of him and external to him. The statement that man is linguistic means that his most immediate and intimate existence has the nature of a verbal utterance. Man's being needs interpretation, as Paul Ricoeur has pointed out, for it is deep, not all on the surface. There is a sense in which man is a word; he does not just use words. In fact, man is able to use words only because his being has the nature of a word.

Words are extensions of the body; they are meaning in matter, a location of presence, embodied presence. Meaning is in words as we are in our bodies, and it is only because we are our bodies that we can "be" our words—or, as it is usually put, mean what we say. We can stand behind our words because our presence overflows them and is more than they can contain, but we choose to stand behind them with our infinite presence because we are also in them. Men are meant to be as good as their word, and hypocrisy is but a disguised version of trying to deny one's bodily location in reality. Double-talk is a way in which a person tries to be in two places at the same time—for we can avoid taking a stand verbally as well as physically.

Young people all over the world today are asking questions about the meaning of life; they are questioning inherited traditions in such areas as sex, politics, the structure of society, and religion. Many parents and statesmen are shocked by the nonconformity of youth, and there are people in the United States who see a Communistic plot to undermine their country in some of the sexual views presently being aired. The real problem, I believe, lies in the fact that for too long the words used by our society have contradicted our bodily lives instead of extending them.

There is a good deal to be said about the possibility of the present sexual "crisis," for example, being a revolution against words instead of against the body. Because our words have been separated from our bodily lives, the young have separated their bodily lives from our words! They are trying to leave behind what appear to them to be purely verbal sanctions and traditions. They have seen verbal traditions to be only verbal. They discover bodily morality in other places: in the treatment of the poor, the suffering, and the under-privileged—places where it always has been in the full Christian tradition. It is a perversion of Christianity to think that bodily morality only concerns sex. When personal dignity is recognized and respected in all its aspects—in our political, economic, and social relations with others—then for the first time in contemporary history we will have the context for sexual morality to be prudently reconsidered in the light of the collective wisdom of the human race.

The distinctively human world is truly said to be a world of words. We define our worlds by our words, and people who learn new words can have new worlds opened to them. We are inserted into reality through language in a manner analagous to the way we are inserted into reality through our bodies. We are born into fields of meaning which precede us in our families and in our cultures; in learning to speak we enter those worlds of meaning. That, in fact, is what education is all about. There is a world of mathematics, political science, philosophy, history, psychology, chemistry, biology, etc. Some of these worlds have worlds within them: experimental and dynamic psychologists, for example, frequently do not speak the same language. As a student I knew two such men who, when they met on their way to class, could only talk about the weather if they wanted to communicate.

Our chapter title is "Body-Meaning." We have seen how man is his body, and we can now move on to illustrations of how man's lived body is also a word. There is no doubt that infants and their mothers communicate before the power of verbal speech has developed in the child. There is a mutual, responsive involvement of mother and child long before the child can talk, and many of the most important things in life are said nonverbally between mother and child in the first months after birth. "Trust" is such a message, and it is communicated from body to body by what can only be described as body-words.

Communication that employs the body as a word is not limited to infants and their mothers however. While infants communicate before they speak, adults often communicate something different by their bodies at the moment they are speaking. When a person politely asks a visitor to stay longer but edges forward in his chair while making his statement, he is saying two different things at the same time—and we know which he means the most! By the same token a wife may say to her husband, "I don't mind if you go," but indicate the very opposite by her facial expression while she is saying it. So frequently are disturbed people caught in such conflicting communication situations, or "double binds" as they have been called, that a school of psychologists has suggested that such communication is either a sign or contributing cause of schizophrenia. When caught in a double bind, the other person does not know what to do; he is wrong whatever he does. No matter which message he acts upon, the verbal or nonverbal one, the person speaking can always claim that he meant the other, and so keep the person to whom he speaks helpless.[2]

Pantomime has been called a universal art, for it speaks to people across language barriers, but it is able to do this only because bodies are indeed words. The body speaks a universal language because every *body* is situated in the world through his body and has a common orientation to life by that fact. We can "read" grief, joy, excitement, and relaxation in another person's body with little difficulty. Attitudes and affections are more catching than ideas just because they influence the body more and so are more easily communicated; there are some people whose presence is depressing no matter what they say with their lips. Their very life is a burden, and they always get their message across.

The fact that we are body-words also helps explain the present enthusiasm for discussion in small groups. While it was once thought that everyone at a meeting should stay together in one room so that all could hear each person's ideas, our increased understanding of group dynamics now leads most large meetings to break up into small discussion groups as soon as possible. Individual participation is better that way. Why? Because in a small group more modes of communication are significant than in a large group. In a small group even "silent communication" allows a person to say something; thus group participation is increased. Large groups tend to be abstractive, or to become the tool of a few highly expressive individuals.

That we can handle things by words is still another indication that words are an extension of our bodies. Man's world is indeed a world of words, for his world is one of highly sophisticated distinctions and nuances. The language of mathematics, especially differential equations, has enabled us to learn and say amazing things about the physical universe. If we were limited to the distinctions we could make by our unaided senses alone, civilization as we know it today could not exist. Even where we are capable of sensory distinctions, words help us sharpen and recognize those distinctions. Most of us would not recognize the difference between mauve and magenta if we did not first know the words, and we know how learning the names of the instruments in an orchestra helps us hear them. Because we can make so many more distinctions by means of words than we can by means of our bodies alone, in many areas of our experience words are a better vehicle of human presence and its capabilities than our bodies are. In this respect our use of words indicates our style of living just as we previously saw our lived bodies doing. Language is a way of living; it is a way of making the world. That is why we can best learn a language by living with the people who use it.

The last similarity between our bodies and language I wish to point out here is that both of them make us communal. Because we are our bodies, I have said we are an outside; this means that we are necessarily related to others just by being ourselves. But nobody owns a language; language is always the possession of a community, for language is a means of communication. If a person had a language that belonged to him alone, he would be an *idiot*, unable to say anything to other people. Our *idio*syncracies are characteristics belonging to us alone that separate us from others. The *idioms* of a language separate it from other languages and are notoriously hard to translate into a different language. Language and words enable human presence to be available to others; words can be used to hide and conceal our motives, but that is not their purpose. They are meant to be means of expression, the means by which we live outside ourselves for what we are.

That nobody owns a language means that our language is always furnished to us by the communities into which we are born or into which we enter through education. A person is not a full member of a community until he can use the language of the community with other members of it. I am a real sports fan or a chemist only when I can talk about sports or chemistry with other fans or chemists. Language even furnishes us with a good model of how individuals should be related to society: individuals depend upon society, but society is meant to be the matrix of individual perfection and growth. The past experience of other people is sedimented in the language systems into which we are born, but with that experience available to us in words of communal significance, we are free to use such words as we choose to try to describe new aspects of experience for others. From the roots of previously used words—and so from past human experience—new words can grow. Through language, society furnishes us with the material of personal freedom.

To conclude these remarks about the role of words in human life, we can say here almost the same things as at the conclusion of our discussion of the body: personal presence is more than words, but we are able to know it to be more only through words and never without words. Human presence needs words in order to be itself, for words, as the extension of body-meaning, anchor us in the world.

We have seen that the body we live is not something to which we must give meaning; it is not an empty container waiting to be filled, for it is the location of our presence. Our bodies are words, always saying something to others whether we wish to speak or not. It is man's nature to be body-meaning and a word; he has no choice about the matter. He does have a choice, however, about what he says as a body-word. Conflicts among men are always conflicts of expression; harmony among men requires expression also.

Christians see Jesus Christ as the fulfillment of man as a body-word, a fulfillment so complete that it amounts to man's recreation. In his own most intimate life in the Trinity, Christian revelation tells us the Father begets a Son and bestows a Spirit; God is the giving of Love within himself. That is why, I have earlier suggested, the loving Father can give and then give to his own giving outside of himself. His first giving is the creation of the universe out of nothing, and the second giving is the recreation of the universe by grace. Recreation (or redemption as it is otherwise known) is God's gift to his gift.

Jesus Christ comes to man as the fulfillment of body and word because, as the prologue of the Gospel according to St. John puts it, in him "the Word became flesh and dwelt among us." (1:14) In Jesus, Christians believe God the Father speaks to man; as the Epistle to the Hebrews says, "in these last days he [the Father] has spoken to us by a Son, whom he appointed the heir of all things. . . . He reflects the glory of

God and bears the very stamp of his nature. . . ." (1:1–3) The
Epistle to the Colossians states that "in him [Christ] the
whole fulness of deity dwells bodily," (2:9) and previously to
that the letter states: "For in him all the fullness of God was
pleased to dwell. . . ." (1:19) The same Epistle says that Christ
Jesus "is the image of the invisible God. . . ." (1:15) To see
Jesus is to see the Father (John 14:9); no one knows the Father
except the Son and those to whom the Son reveals him. (Matt.
11:27 and Luke 10:22)

Strong words from the heart of the Christian tradition.
What do they mean?

They mean that in Jesus Christ the mysterious and different personal presence of the Father is located for man in
human terms. Belief in the Incarnation does not mean that
God the Father is present to man for the first time, for man
is nothing without the presence of the Father; the Father is
always present to his creation or it would not exist. The
Incarnation means that in Jesus Christ the Father is present
to us *as we are,* not simply for what he is—infinite difference
from us. The Word of the Father is the Father's expression
of himself; the Word is the Father's exteriorization. Jesus
Christ is the Father's ex-pression of himself as man; that is
what is meant when the Word is said to have become flesh.
In the Incarnation, the Word of God does not just use man
but is the Father's presence *as* man. In Jesus Christ the Father becomes present in the world in a way so radically new
that it creates a new world: a new order of bodies and words
is established from the inside out in the Word made flesh.

It is now time to turn to the consequences of the new
location of God's presence in the world through Jesus. What
difference does his new manner of presence make? It re-
defines the nature of our lived bodies, and it gives new significance—life—to our words.

By nature our bodies center our lived worlds. When the
Word was made flesh, however, the human body received a

new explicit meaning. As the Gospel according to St. John tells it, "God so loved the world that he *gave* his only Son, that whoever believes in him should not perish but have eternal life. For God *sent* the Son into the world . . . that the world might be saved through him." (3:16 f.—italics mine) In chapter 8 of the same Gospel, Jesus is reported to have said, "If God were your Father, you would love me, for I proceeded and came forth from God; I came not of my own accord, but he *sent* me." (v.42—italics mine)

It is because God loves the world that he sent his Son. Too frequently Christians have paid attention only to what the Son did after he arrived in the world; certainly the importance of what Christ did in the world cannot be overestimated, but we must also pay attention to the "that" of the sending. The Son was sent, and the Father is present to us in him; it was because God wanted to be present with us *as we are* that he sent his Son into the world. It was only as present in the world that the Son went on to express himself in a certain way in his life and death. What Christ did was the result of the overflowing of God's presence in him, but he had to be filled with God before the overflowing could take place. Similarly we must be aware of God's presence to us before that presence can knowingly overflow us.

That God sent his Son to be present with us is the mark of his love for us. The Son came when "the Word became flesh" and the presence of God was located in the world through a body. In Christianity, then, the body is the body-word of love. The body is unmistakably seen to be the gift of love and is sent to be the means of love.

The difficulty we too frequently have as Christians is to make our bodies ends in themselves. We want peace for the body's sake: the condition of our bodies is what upsets us the most and what we most worry about. However, for a Christian, the body is only—but always—a means to more love. That is the body's new definition: the means of love.

Christians are bodies for the same reason the Word became flesh, i.e., because they are sent by the Father to show
his love for the world in the world. A Christian's body is the
center of his experience, but it is not the sole center of his
world. The body of Jesus Christ centers a Christian's world,
as the body of the beloved always centers a lover's world. If
Tom loves Mary *she* centers his world.

Because we are members of the human community in
virtue of our bodies—because our bodies have an outside and
therefore constantly relate us to others—our bodies are
meant to be our ever-present means of expressing God's love
for all men. Christians, realizing that they are creatures sent
by the Father in the name of Christ, realize that their bodies
are always points of departure and bridges beyond themselves instead of ends in themselves. Teresa of Avila said in
the sixteenth century that love, not consolations, is the important thing for a Christian. That is the key to the Christian
understanding of the body.

As creatures sent by the Father, men's purpose is to proclaim the love that locates them in the world. They can do
it only by going beyond themselves, but that is easy for Christians, for "through Christ our consolation overflows." (2 Corinthians 1:5, NEB) As first consoled by the love of God in
Christ, Christians cannot contain their consolation. The presence of God is that way. Love can literally fill the world if
men will let it affect the body, for then it will be thick and
the same stuff as the world; Christian love is not something
spiritual that cannot be seen, for Christian love is Jesus Christ
in the flesh. Love that makes no difference in the world is not
love.

The human body is redefined in Christ as the means of love
—and nothing less than the Father's creative love at that.
What can we say now about the new significance Christ gives
us as words?

First of all, since we have seen that we are body-words,

what our bodies are determines what we shall be as words. Christians are meant to be effective words—the expression —of God's creative love in the world. The important point is never to forget that we *are* words; we do not just use words as something beyond us. To be created is to be meaning even before we search for meaning, for our creation is our "being spoken" by God. We *are* expression instead of having to search for something foreign to us to bring to expression; the latter produces anxiety, for we are constantly on the spot, while the former brings peace.

The trouble is, we are God's word before we are ready to speak. That is how close God's meaning is to us; that is the meaning of being a creature. Because being God's word is a gift, not something we earn or attain, we must be it where we are, for we are it already. Because we do not work toward it, we cannot be separated from it.

To realize that as creatures we are body-words is to realize the immediacy of God in our lives. That is the purpose of the "body theology" we are developing. We are body-subjects, location, love, before all else. Before theory, problems, success, defeat. *That* is the way we are with God and that is why we can be at home with him. The immediacy of our lived bodies is the immediacy of his meaning in our lives. His meaning, as our bodies, is the condition of all else in the world.

I said a short time ago that the Father's presence in the world in Jesus gave new significance to our words. A better way of putting it is to say that in Jesus we as words are life.

It is frequently said that the fear all men have of death is the fear of annihilation. The thought or feeling of returning to nonbeing frightens us. Upon a better analysis, however, the dread of death is the dread of being rendered completely passive and inexpressive, not of returning to nonbeing. We have no idea of nonbeing; it is something we cannot conceive and certainly cannot imagine. But we *are* expression and we do know what it means to be unable to initiate expression. That is the feeling of death as we can now know it.

Death is where we can say nothing; in it our words—and we are words—are rendered passive. Death is fearful because it is complete passivity. Death is possible for us because we are creatures. That we can be rendered completely passive is the ultimate indication that we are created, i.e., that even our most active being is a *gift* from Another.

Jesus Christ, the incarnate Word of God, is identity through death. God's Word, instead of being rendered passive by death as we are, is able to say something about death even *while passing throught it*. The Word remains active and expressive through death and so does not die. The Word says about death what we want to say but cannot: that death is overcome—that it is not final.

The gift of God to man in Christ is that if men will live their bodies as Christ's word in the world, Christ's body will be their Word through death. That is the meaning of the resurrection of the body: as present to God with Christ in the world, God's presence will be our expression through death. In speaking here of the resurrection of Christ's body I am referring to the body in its fundamental sense as the principle of personal location; this is not an attempt to describe its specific nature. The resurrection of the body means that even after death we will have some type of location in reality similar to that now supplied us by the body; in other words, the significance of personal life as we now know it located in the world will continue. That is why our present life is so important for us: it is the key to life everlasting. In the presence of God we can overcome death. Christ can be said to overcome the world and death because he brings the meaning of the presence of God to the world and to death from beyond them.

The best descriptive data about man with which we are furnished today indicate that man as a person is radically *temporal* in his constitution, being a constant synthesis of the modalities of time known as past, present, and future; he is most himself through a *specific location in the world,* which location originates through his body; his being is *intentional,* always referring beyond itself and thus always correlative to a world; his being is *linguistic,* a type of being which permits and requires interpretation; as a person he is always a *whole,* never merely a conjunction of discrete parts; he is *communal,* not able to be himself by himself.

If the nature of the Christian life and of the church can be seen in immediate relation to such themes as I have just mentioned, themes which lie at the foundation of all human meaning, what once might have been thought of as isolated religious issues will take on new significance. If, for example, the Christian life can be understood in terms that are coextensive with "human being," then that life can be understood in a manner which makes an immediate difference to being human. If life in the church can be brought into focus by being directly related to the ultimate context of human meaning, it will not appear to be an issue which ought to concern only a few; instead, it will be seen to be a perfection of the human condition which none should escape. Not "whether" but "how" one will participate in the fabric of the Christian life will then be the first question people should ask themselves.

The ingredients of the world are the ingredients of Christianity. As was previously noted, something big is going on in the world today, and we are part of it. The only question is, "What part shall we play?" There are some people of a fatalistic persuasion who think the course of the world inevitable. Christians believe that with creative use of the structure of a history which often appears inevitable, the results need not be inevitable. The Christian community, in other words, is one of hope.

It is not that we are to push our bodies around in meaningful ways. Our bodies *are* meaning! That is the Christian message. Our bodies are words. Christian meaning is something we walk into and which employs our whole being. The traditional name for such meaning is "sacrament." Over the centuries the Christian sacraments have lost their full significance because people, trying to protect their significance, restricted their use and interpretation. The sacraments were thought to be so precious that they were all too frequently kept in jewel boxes called churches and isolated from the general conditions of mankind. This is especially true of the most inclusive sacrament of Christendom, the Holy Eucharist. It appeared to be the special possession of the priestly class, who "put it on"—often magnificently—for other Christians to attend and observe. People went to "hear mass."

Actually, the sacraments are something all men walk into with the vunerability of an exposed body. Sacramental truth is not an unlocated, eternal truth we try to assimilate in our lives or try to bring to ourselves. It calls us to be our bodyselves. It is something into which we step, and it keeps us stepping. The sacraments are the same mode of meaning our bodies are; they are meaning we must live, not just think about.

The same is true of the church. If what I have been suggesting in this chapter is true, we can understand the church as the body of Christ, to use the description of St. Paul, only if we understand it as *God's project in the world.*

To change the present into God's future, according to the promise God has given all men in Christ's resurrection in the past, is the project, the pro-ject, that defines the church. Only that project is the living body of Christ, and only people engaged in that project are living members of the body. We must remember that Christ has no dead body. The body each one of us lives is mission to make one kind of world rather than another. If we are living members of Christ's body, our mission is to make God's world through our bodies; just as we saw to be the case with love (which is really the same thing), a Christianity that does not change the world is no Christianity at all.

We have seen that a project is future-oriented, goal-directed. What is the goal of God's project, the church, in the world? Nothing less than man sharing the divine life! We are intended to experience the Son's intimacy with the Father in the warmth of the Spirit. The beginning and end of God's project is interpersonal relations, his internal life of love.

If the interpersonal relations we know as Father, Son, and Holy Spirit are the beginning and end of our existence, interpersonal relations, not things, are meant to be the beginning, middle, and end of our lives as human beings in this world. But to relate personally to someone, we have seen that we must first locate him. Here the body comes in again. Lovers want their bodies located in each other's arms. Collection agencies have built up thriving businesses locating people for their clients. Letters, telephone calls, interviews, television, radio, trysts, property rights, and civil rights are all ways we locate each other through our bodies. A person without a body-principle is no longer a person in this world—or anywhere else, I would say. Any kind of personal relation in this world has some bodily dimension.

Our ultimate goal of sharing in the interpersonal life of God forces us to bodily respect, bodily humility, and bodily help in our relations to each other in the world. There is no other way we can have, or provide for, interpersonal relations. What kind of involvement prior to bodily concern can there be among people who can claim to be Christians only because they are members of the body of Christ?

One body of Christ, one project of God, one goal of man: these three coincide. We try to kill Christ again if we do not bodily testify to the unity of all men in him. In him all men are projected toward one future; the task of men who are members of his body is to witness to the oneness of that future in the present, which means to change the present.

The Holy Eucharist is a sacrament of the body and offers people who participate in it the fullest body-meaning a Christian can know. In the Eucharist, Christians believe they receive the Body of Christ, who is the Word of God, in the midst of the paradigmatic expression of the Christian community. Body, word, and community! Given to men as a gift from God, the Eucharist nevertheless has secular roots, roots that are identical with the constitutive principles of man's personal being. Man's most immediate experience of himself in the world is thus seen to be the key to his understanding the Eucharist. God made use of such themes as the *"Body* of Christ," the *"Word* of God," and the *"People* of Israel" in the revelatory process precisely because of their meaning value in human experience. The Eucharist is a total way of being in the world, for it consecrates the bodily, linguistic, and communal dimensions of man's being, out of which his experience of the world is made possible. The means by which man experiences his world become, in the Eucharist, the means by which God lets man help create His world.

In the sense in which man must be body, word, and community wherever he is, eucharistic significance is never absent from his life. Such significance is coextensive with his experience in the world; it is not by employing a weakly extended metaphor that he is charged to "see" the Eucharist everywhere. His very being is the presence of the eucharistic "elements." Consecration occurs through thanksgiving, and wherever a man thankfully aligns his will with God's, essential eucharistic participation through body, word, and community is going on. That is the meaning of the Christian life. Seeing the Eucharist everywhere does not weaken the Eucharist's significance and make life easier; if anything, the Eucharist's universality enriches the significance of life and makes it harder. Life is harder because constancy is called for and responsibility increased. The abstraction and isolation of issues from the intimate eucharistic will of Christ becomes impossible. Everything is then crucial, not just a few things. *That* is eucharistic living; the demand to grow and the grace of God's eucharistic gift are found everywhere.

Contemporary anthropology, especially owing to the insights of Martin Heidegger, shows that man always exists in relation to the world and to other human beings and that the dimensions of time are constitutive of his being. There is a time we live which is more primary to us than the time we measure by clocks and calendars—the time we *are*. Lived time supplies dimensionality to personal existence; everything truly personal is temporal, and everything most significantly temporal for man is personal. Because of the temporal character of man's being, only he makes history. A human life is one of temporal synthesis, and what cannot creatively synthesize the dimensions of time cannot be historical in the first meaning of that term. History, therefore, can be attributed to the nonhuman world only in a derivative sense; things become historical for man only because of the role they play in his life.

Because of the emphasis on the future in so much contemporary theology, the essential openness of man's being and his creaturely relation to the Father are never lost sight of in it, as they have been in much past theology. The present emphasis on the primacy of the historically concrete over static abstractions coincides with the type of reality we discover ourselves to be as maturing persons in the world. Thus our religion can be real in our maturing lives. God's first encounter with us is a total relationship involving every aspect of our being. God creates a history so new in Christ that the history is known to be possible to man only because it actually happened. Witness and testimony are that history's only proof. God's future creates man's possibilities, which is the reason man can be himself only with God.

In temporal terms, the difficulty too often made in Christianity is denying its historicity. Even those who accept Jesus as the Christ want to be saved by their theories about him; they want redemption, in other words, through what they think. But people can become Christians only by letting Jesus happen to them; they must let him be present to them for the absolutely different presence he is. In that presence they will be called beyond their theories to a personal relationship, and only in such a relationship can they become so new as persons that they are recreated.

Sacraments are a mode of meaning as historical and temporal as Christianity itself. Sacraments take time to do, and they make time by what they do. The temporal action of the sacraments shows how time should be used. In the historical action of every Holy Eucharist, for example, the church, as the body of Christ on earth, incorporates all the faithful who participate in it, and the physical elements of bread and wine, into the historical life-style of Jesus Christ himself. By freely coming to do in time what Jesus freely did in time in the upper room and on Calvary—i.e., give himself for others —human beings and the physical elements of the universe through which they express themselves are given a meaning which can be supplied only by the presence of God.[3] Identifying themselves in time with the temporal activity of Jesus Christ, Christians become the presence of his body—his lived body, his life-style or project—in the world. They thus become agents of redemption in the world and can live with the freedom and joy that results from overcoming death.

Whenever human beings use time (and they *are* time,

remember), they are participating in the most intimate life of Jesus and his presence with the Father. All the sacraments, and especially the Eucharist, show that the "regular time" that bores us and in which our minds wander is the vehicle of God's redemptive, creative action. Consecration takes time, and all time is meant to be consecrating. Christians go to the Eucharist to learn how to use time in God's way and to offer their time to God in Christ Jesus; as a result of the presence of the glorified Christ in the new mode of his body effected by the eucharistic consecration, God allows his people to participate in their future in the present! The future the Father intends for his creatures becomes their food, giving them the strength of the future to change their present.

People draw meaning out of what they *do*, which fact enables the sacraments to be a source of *hope* in their lives. Jesus Christ told his followers to do something in his name: "Do this in remembrance of me," he said. (1 Corinthians 11:24) That action is the hope of all who trust in him. By doing, believers move into time with their whole being, and time we have repeatedly seen is man's being. How different a sacramental life is from just thinking about time! Time does not threaten a person who lives sacramentally, for he feels that he belongs in time; his hope is in time through time. He does not try to escape time and the decision for which it calls.

The Christian sacraments are something men do, but they are not the "nonexpressive behavior" psychologists have noted in their studies of anxiety. Christians find infinite meaning in sacramental action because, as actions *given* to them by the one who revealed the Father in the world, the sacraments locate the infinite presence of God in the world. Their meaning for man is, then, both mysteriously infinite and bodily moving.

Notes

1. Arthur A. Vogel, *The Next Christian Epoch* (New York: Harper & Row, 1966), and especially *Is the Last Supper Finished: Secular Light on a Sacred Meal* (New York: Sheed & Ward, 1968), *passim.*

2. Cf. Paul Watzlawick, Janet Beavin, and Don Jackson, *Pragmatics of Human Communication: A Study of Interactional Patterns, Pathologies, and Paradoxes* (New York: W. W. Norton & Co. 1967), *passim.*

3. Cf. Vogel, *Is the Last Supper Finished?*, chap. 3.

.6.

The Way We Act and the Peace We Seek

To endorse personal religion today is embarrassing if one does not know the presence of God. "Personal religion" is the "old stuff" that no longer sells; it smacks of the pietism that preached itself to death and left the world as it found it.

There has been much talk about personal religion in these pages, and I have tried to give it a thoroughly contemporary and at the same time systematically adequate justification. I am enthusiastic about personal religion, but also realize that too frequently in the past what has gone by that name kept Christianity from being an effective agent in the world. Reaction has now set in. In the field of religion, social concern is presently battling against personal concern—yet this is another war that should not be fought. Certainly the new recognition of social responsibility many people have discovered in their religious lives must be encouraged and extended to still more people; the discovery of the social responsibility we have toward each other has just begun, but social concern and personal religion cannot be separated. To attempt to do so is to understand wrongly both the nature of a person and the nature of society. Persons are themselves only in community; we have seen that they always have communal aspects, so a consideration of them and their problems can always start from either the social or the individual point of view. But a consideration must start somewhere, and there is good reason to start an examination of religion where we have, with its meaning in our most immediate experience of reality. In my own view, when personal religion is fully itself it is the way of recreating the world, for persons can be themselves only in a world. What we need is full personal religion, personal religion filled with the presence of God; *that* presence, we have seen, must overflow us into the world.

Humility and peace are time-honored themes of personal religion, but of the two peace is more intriguing to contemporary minds because so many interesting people of different backgrounds presently discuss and seek it. Peace is a viable contemporary goal. Humility is not much discussed in a society struggling to maintain—or often establish for the first time—the *rights* of many of its citizens. A call for humility today sounds to many like the paternalism of yesterday, which amounted to slavery to those for whom humility seemed the most appropriate virtue.

But for anyone who has experienced the absolute difference of the presence of God as I have tried to describe it, humility is a necessary qualification of the way he acts, and peace turns out to be something quite different from what we now hear so much talk about. In any case, we cannot avoid discussing humility and peace in the approach here taken to religion, for they are essentially involved in the dynamics of a creature who, as a person, can know God as a Person.

We, as creatures, are dynamic, for we are created to create. We are able to create, I have tried to show, because we are constantly called by the presence of God beyond our present selves.

Presence makes the difference.

Words which are trite in themselves become filled with meaning when they are the location of personal presence. "I love you," is the only illustration we need to secure the point.

So much religious talk strikes us as quaint, if not trite, just because the presence of God is not found in it. We hear it as if in an echo chamber; the words are merely noises bouncing against the walls of an empty room. The words may once have been filled with personal presence and backed by that same presence, but now they are empty and ineffective.

Talk about humility often sounds that way today; it is an echo from the past. But if this is the way it sounds to us, it is because we have lost our awareness of God's presence. In the presence of God no virtue is easier or more natural to us. Interestingly enough, it does for people who have it what the psychiatrist Viktor Frankl claims to achieve through "paradoxical intention," as we shall see shortly.

The more one reads the great Christian literature, and the more one studies the great Christian lives, the more he becomes convinced of the primacy of humility. It is the virtue most suitable for creatures to have. To show its centrality to the Christian tradition, we need only note three sayings attributed to Jesus Christ in the Gospel according to St. Matthew: "Whoever humbles himself like this child, he is the greatest in the kingdom of heaven." (18:4) "Blessed are the poor in spirit, for theirs is the kingdom of heaven." (5:3) "He who is greatest among you shall be your servant; whoever exalts himself will be humbled, and whoever humbles himself will be exalted." (23:11f.)

Humility is nothing but the realization of ourselves for what we are. The most convincing empirical evidence we have—birth and death—show that no ultimate rights or powers originate in us; we have our beginning and end in someone other than ourselves. How absurd to try to contradict our beginning and end by the way we live in between them!

Because humility is a realization of what we *are,* it is never something we can sufficiently acquire or excessively go beyond. It is us; it does not *belong* to us. If we ever feel that we have it or wonder whether we have it, we have to step outside of it to judge or admire it. But to step outside of it is to lose it. It is not a thing, a possession; it cannot be attained or displayed. It can only be discovered by others—and lived by us.

I remember with what admiration the publisher of an internationallly known theologian remarked that, in the course of a private conversation, the theologian once told him that humility was the crown of the Christian virtues. Actually, it is not so much the crown as the foundation of Christian virtues; it is the crown because it is the foundation.

Teresa of Avila, whom I have briefly mentioned once before, was one of the most attractive and interesting persons ever to follow Jesus Christ. This simple woman had profound psychological insight, and was so vital and active in her religion that in spite of her now past cultural location she has much to say to people of today. Her descriptions of the spirtiual life are especially valuable because she never lost sight of its dynamism and complexity. Although there are stages through which a person passes in his life with God, she realized that such development is never mechanical: thus a person is never neatly in one category or stage at a time. In her greatest book, the *Interior Castle,* she used a castle "made of a single diamond or of very clear crystal" as an image for the soul.[1] Within it, she continued, there are many rooms and mansions.* But these dwelling places are not laid

*This English word (here and below—something of an anomaly when applied to the precincts of a castle—is explained in a translator's note. The Spanish noun derives simply from the verb "to dwell," but more important, is a direct allusion to John 14:2, "In my Father's house are many mansions: if it were not so I would have told you" AV—the translator's reason, no doubt,

out end to end, so that a person can pass from one to another in a straight line in order to reach the most intimate presence of God. Instead, God is in the center of the castle, and different mansions or rooms are above, below, and at each side of him. She distinguishes seven principal mansions in the book, yet at its conclusion she says that within each one she has described are contained many more, themselves "above and below and around, with lovely gardens and fountains and things so delectable that you will want to lose yourselves in praise of the great God Who created it in His image and likeness."[2]

Teresa held that those who are praying, be it much or little, should not be subject to "undue constraint or limitation."[3] Dialogue can never be itself if it is artificially constrained from the outside. A person should be allowed to roam through the mansions as he will and can.

Nevertheless, there is a sound order in approaching God. Proud people must not think that on a moment's notice, or no notice at all, they can jump into the center of the castle and experience God in glowing ecstasy. Still, no person must be compelled to remain in any one room for a long period of time—with the single exception of the room of self-knowledge. This is otherwise known as the room of humility. It is the first of the castle's mansions, and even after describing the seventh mansion (that of spiritual marriage, the highest perfection of man), Teresa concludes by saying that nothing is more important than humility for entering *any* mansion.

In speaking to this point she goes on to say:

"For the foundation of this whole edifice, as I have said, is humility, and, if you have not true humility, the Lord will not wish it to reach any great height: in fact, it is for your own good that it should not; if it did, it would fall to the ground. Therefore . . . if you wish to lay good foundations, each of you must try to be the least of all, and the

for keeping the slightly odd English rendering, which for the reader, however, carries a clear reference to the Gospel as another word would not.

slave of God, and must seek a way and means to please and serve all your companions. If you do that, it will be of more value to you than to them and your foundation will be so firmly laid that your Castle will not fall.

I repeat that if you have this in view you must not build upon foundations of prayer and contemplation alone, for, unless you strive after the virtues and practise them, you will never grow to be more than dwarfs. God grant that nothing worse than this may happen—for, as you know, anyone who fails to go forward begins to go back, and love, I believe, can never be content to stay for long where it is.

You may think that I am speaking about beginners, and that later on one may rest: but, as I have already told you, the only repose that these souls enjoy is of an interior kind; of outward repose they get less and less, and they have no wish to get more. . . .[4]

Teresa's keen insight into the psychology of the Christian life—that too much concern with ourselves can keep us from knowing ourselves—is shown in the following:

Humility must always be doing its work like a bee making its honey in the hive: without humility all will be lost. Still, we should remember that the bee is constantly flying about from flower to flower and in the same way, believe me, the soul must sometimes emerge from self-knowledge and soar aloft in meditation upon the greatness and the majesty of its God. Doing this will help it to realize its own baseness better than thinking of its own nature. . . . For although, as I say, it is through the abundant mercy of God that the soul studies to know itself, yet one can have too much of a good thing, as the saying goes, and believe me, we shall reach much greater heights of virtue by thinking upon the virtue of God than if we stay in our own little plot of ground and tie ourselves down to it completely.

I do not know if I have explained this clearly: self-knowledge is so important that, even if you were raised right up to the heavens, I should like you never to relax your cultivation of it; so long as we are on this earth, nothing matters more to us than humility. And so I repeat that it is a very good thing—excellent, indeed—to begin by entering the room where humility is acquired rather then by flying off to the other rooms. For that is the way to make progress, and, if we have a safe, level road to walk along, why should we desire wings to fly? Let us rather try to get the greatest possible profit out of walking. As I see it, we shall never succeed in knowing ourselves unless we seek to know God: let us think of His greatness and then come back to our own baseness; by looking at His purity we shall see our foulness; by meditating upon His humility, we shall see how far we are from being humble.[5]

The inconsistencies of our daily moods and inclinations were also known to Teresa; she saw their cure in the virtue of humility. There were times, she said, that she felt "extremely detached" from the world, and yet when a test suddenly presented itself she felt such wordly attachment that she scarcely knew herself. There were times she felt—and proved—her courage in serving God, yet on other days she felt she could do nothing for his sake if she met any opposition to it, even in such a small matter as "killing an ant!" Again, she said that there were times when other people's remarks to or about her didn't bother her at all, but on another occasion a single harsh word would cause her great dismay. She knew that she was not alone in these problems, and we know it too. She knew a solution, however, that many of us do not know.

To be told that we muct act in humility and that humility is the "first" of the virtues is another strand of the Christian tradition that sounds distasteful to modern ears. The Christian doctrine of creation, we have seen, sounds equally repellent to those same ears, and there is a reason why both doctrines sound the same, for the primacy of humility in human life depends on the fact of our creation. True humility is not self-depreciation, morbidity, or weakness; it is self-appreciation, the acceptance of the fact that we as persons depend completely on the presence of God.

Humility is not quiescent passivity; it is the using of so

much of ourselves with God that our status with men becomes unimportant. We all want security, but Christian security does not show itself in self-sufficiency or boastful independence. Christian security makes a man humble, not proud. If our security is in God, it is he, not we who must show. Humility is extreme personal involvement and commitment, but first with God and then, because of him, with men. Here is no question of temporal priorities, for we have already seen that the presence of God can only be known through the presence of men. Concerned here, instead, are priorities of personal discernment: once God's presence is discerned in human presence, his presence must be the reason we act the way we do with men. The joyfulness and freedom that characterize truly humble people is the proof that humility is a virtue, not personal weakness or a social disease.

Jean-Paul Sartre tells in his autobiography how he used to turn to humility in order to avoid humiliation. When he felt ashamed of something he had done as a young boy, he made monstrous faces at himself in a mirror; if he could convince himself that he was a monster, his remorse could turn to pity. Most of us are good at similar tricks, but we try to come off as social benefactors instead of monsters in practicing them. Seeing out of the corner of his eye another car approaching the same intersection, a driver increases the speed of his car to the corner. If it becomes apparent that he will lose the undeclared race, rather than admit defeat he assumes an attitude of great unconcern and courtesy, perhaps smiling and motioning the other driver to proceed ahead of him. What he tries to pass off as courtesy is merely a disguise his pride assumes in a last-minute effort to remain intact. If the other driver is a woman, his assumed courtesy may know no bounds!

Sitting in a large room listening to a boring lecture, we are apt idly to look around and let our glance fall arbitrarily where it will. If someone leaves his seat and walks down the aisle, our eyes follow him with a blank, abstract stare. If *we* decide to leave the room for a drink of water, however, we hesitate. Other people will stare at us just as we have stared at them. They will pay no more real attention to us than we paid to them, but now we tend to read our most intimate being into their stares. Because we project our attachment to ourselves into these glances, they become so personal that we hesitate to leave our seat.

Not only is personal religion not opposed to social concern, as we saw at the beginning of this chapter, but the virtues of personal religion are necessary to make true social concern possible. Humility may furnish a surprising case in point. Pride isolates us from others, making it impossible for us to accept them as they are or to help them in *their* need. The egotist, seeing a sick or deformed person, or someone in pain or bleeding—to take obvious examples—can only react against the distasteful sight. Even though he sees disease in another, he can only think about it in relation to himself. Does not a similar reaction explain people's self-conscious behavior at funerals? We could be lying there! Francis of Assisi said that before his complete commitment to God it was a very difficult thing for him to look at lepers. After his conversion he embraced them, ministered to them, and even ate out of common dishes with them. The poor and undereducated today threaten large masses of our established citizenry just as thoroughly, but in less obvious ways, as the physically sick.

From the point of view of an insecure ego, everything unfortunate that happens to others is regarded as a possible threat to *me*. I see myself in their situation, and a cold shudder is the reward for my trouble. Humility enables us to make contact with others and so to minister to them. *They* become our first thought, and help for them becomes our first reaction. We have seen earlier that we project a style of living around us. The concern we project into the world—for ourselves or for others—vitally determines the way the world affects us: humility, by making it possible for us not to react against the misfortune of others, makes it possible for us to love them in all circumstances.

Pride, the disguise of insecurity, is the source of anxiety; nothing cuts anxiety like humility. The humble person is free because he is released from bondage to himself. Many neurotic people are plagued by what has been called "anticipatory anxiety." They anticipate something in the future with such dread that their anticipation actually brings about the thing they fear. Dr. Viktor Frankl has given the example of a person who is so afraid of blushing when he enters a room filled with people that he actually blushes.

On the other hand, strangely enough, we find that an excessive intention to do something, or an excessive attention to what is being done, frequently prevents us from doing what we most want to do. Think of the person who cannot go to sleep because he is trying so desperately to sleep. A vicious circle of self is formed in all these cases, which makes the image of a snake eating its tail a very apt symbol for this type of neurosis.

In treating such neurotic circle formations, Dr. Frankl has developed a technique called "paradoxical intention." In it the patient actively intends the very thing he fears. Once the fear is replaced by the "paradoxical wish" the anxiety has nothing upon which to feed. In order to be successful, however, Dr. Frankl writes that this procedure "must make use of the specifically human capacity for self-detachment inherent in a sense of humor. This basic capacity to detach one form oneself is actualized whenever . . . 'paradoxical intention' is applied. At the same time, the patient is enabled to put himself at a distance from his own neurosis."[6] Where the patient has discovered a meaning for his life as a whole— when there are no gaps of meaning in certain areas of it—

Dr. Frankl has found that his simple technique has produced quick and lasting results. The neurotic, circular symptoms accompanying anticipation and intention, described above, are elicited by the meaninglessness of life; the symptoms can be counteracted by paradoxical intention when the patient is reoriented "toward his specific vocation and mission in life."

Frankl continues, "It is not the neurotic's self-concern, whether pity or contempt, which breaks the circle formation; the cue to cure is self-commitment!"[7]

Paradoxical intention is a means of cutting oneself off from himself when he is overly concerned about himself. It can thus be seen as a psychological implementation of the attitudes of trust and humility. Dr. Frankl mentions the self-detachment intrinsic to a sense of humor and states that it is necessary for this technique to work. But humility and humor come from the same root; without humility a person cannot laugh at himself. As a psychological tool, paradoxical intention needs a context within which to work; that is why Dr. Frankl also stresses the necessity of the patient's having a meaningful life-outlook. Actually, trust and humility supply the context which allows paradoxical intention to be successful. But if trust and humility are present in a person in their fullness, they make paradoxical intention unnecessary by preventing neurosis from occurring in the first place. If one lives outside of himself with God, he does not need to feed on himself in anxiety.

Humility and trust go together. Each is an attitude in itself, but because each is so basic it affects every aspect of a person's life. All the dimensions of the Christian life flow into one another, enrich one another, lead to one another. To make a real beginning anywhere in it is to be on the right road to everything in it.

This inseparableness of the dimensions of Christian living may be illustrated from the well-known thirteenth chapter of St. Paul's First Epistle to the Corinthians. On a quick reading it may appear that Paul is speaking only of the familiar triumvirate of faith, hope, and charity (love). His conclusion is that "the greatest of these is love"—but observe how love is described: it is said to be "patient and kind . . . not jealous or boastful . . . not arrogant or rude. Love does not insist on its own way; it is not irritable or resentful; it does not rejoice at wrong, but rejoices in the right. Love bears all things, believes all things, hopes all things, endures all things." (Vss. 4–7) In describing love, St. Paul has in fact given a detailed description of humility; one is not found without the other.

The mutual reference and interdependence of the various aspects of the religious life become readily apparent as soon as we try to grow in trust or humility. The latter may be said to "get us to where we are" (for pride always makes us think we are more than we are), while trust "gets us to God." Yet God is always where we are—we cannot be ourselves without discovering him; and it is only in his presence that we discover our true selves. Trust and humility are really dimensions of each other. Their necessary interrelation may also be seen when we analyze the difficulties people have in cultivating them. The problem is: either we do not have humility enough to trust, or we do not have trust enough to be humble.

Peace, I have said, is more intriguing to the contemporary mind than humility; more people see the need for it than for humility, although close scrutiny shows that a person cannot genuinely have one without the other. We live in great turmoil today; in fact, it has been suggested that the present rate of change in the world so surpasses our level of tolerance that we are in the midst of a national nervous breakdown. In such times nothing is more striking than a man of peace. Throughout the history of mankind men of true personal peace have been singularly compelling. Great religious leaders have always had this quality about them; it was a mark of the revelation they brought. Contemporary Eastern gurus attract followers for the same reason. Peace speaks of the perfection of the person; it affirms completion, wholeness, fulfillment, and consolation in the midst of life.

There is and always has been a great thirst for peace in the world. It is currently much symbolized, extolled, demonstrated for; its need has been endlessly proclaimed, but it has not yet been achieved. One thing at least is certain: peace cannot be imposed on individuals or nations. Power blocks may balance each other in international politics, but the peace people need cannot be defined in the negative terms of standoff and survival alone. Peace is the *presence*, not the absence, of something.

It is interesting to discover the definition of peace offered by many of its most vocal contemporary advocates. By many young members of the "peace movement" it is said to be each person "doing his own thing." This essentially means freedom to do what one wants. Such a definition, of course, makes it no more than a misleading label for anarchy.

There is an important philosophical strain in Western history, however, that may be approached through the definition of peace as each person doing his own thing. That strain of thought equates peace with justice and is deeply rooted in Western culture by its presentation in Plato's *Republic*. It can be, and has been, reasonably maintained that there can be no peace among men without justice and that where justice prevails peace should be found.

In the dialogue recounted by Plato in the *Republic*, Socrates and some of his friends are discussing the nature of justice as a personal virtue. In order to facilitate the discussion, the suggestion is made that justice be examined in the state, where it exists on a larger scale and is therefore easier to see. The fallacy of arguing from the nature of a political community composed of a number of individuals with complete personalities of their own to the complex nature of a single individual need not detain us here, but we shall be aware of it in our discussion. Socrates' contention through the pen of Plato is that different groups of people perform different functions in society: workmen, merchants, artisans, and craftsmen supply the material needs of life; soldiers protect the citizens of a country; and wise governors are needed to rule the state. The cardinal virtues of temperance, courage, and wisdom apply to every class within the state, but Plato suggests that there is a special identification of workers with temperance, of soldiers with courage, and of governors with wisdom.

Two tenets of Plato are especially important. First of all he held that justice, the fourth cardinal virtue, applies to the state as a whole and is achieved when each class within a state does its proper job by itself without external interference. Secondly, although Plato defines justice in terms of each doing his own "thing," the thing to be done in each case is a virtuous activity. It is a function necessary for a fully human life, and it involves the way a person habituates and disciplines himself to act within time. Aristotle developed this train of thought even more, and it is here that Plato and Aristotle differ so radically from some of our contemporaries who appear to use their ideas. The Greeks knew that men in the world are temporal, and that there can be no justice without the disciplined use of time; "each doing his own business" is not a license for anyone to do anything he wants any time he wants. For the Greeks, peace is a harmony of virtue throughout society and within each person in it.

As the concept of justice was developed by Aristotle and the philosophical tradition bearing his name, it was said always to involve either an equality or proportionality between at least two persons. In the justice of commerce and business, equality is aimed for: in a commerical transaction a person should get value equal to the price he pays for a product. Equality between buyer and seller, regardless of who the buyer and seller are, is the only just standard. Infringements on such justice are rampant in our marketplaces today, making consumer protection a major national issue. We need manufacturers who will read Aristotle as well as profit statements.

In proportional justice more factors enter into consideration than in commercial justice. What a person happens to have in his hand or pocket is not the sole criterion for justice; what he is morally worth and *should* have also enter the picture. There is justice possible among unequals as well as equals. In such cases reward should be proportional to merit; greater recognition should be given for greater service. Military decorations and peace prizes are attempts at such justice. "From each according to his ability and to each according to his need" is an attempt to embody this type of justice throughout society.

For many centuries the theological vocabulary of the major part of Western Christendom was based on the Greek philosophers to whom we are referring, but even so Christians were quick to see that in relations between God and man there can be no justice of proportionality—let alone justice of equality.Not only is man not equal to God; there is not even any proportion between man and God. Man *completely* depends on God, so there is nothing in the name of justice that he can demand from God. Man's whole being is a gift; it is not something merited or earned. That is the meaning of the doctrine of creation. The most religious person in the world cannot be just in his relations with God, because God cannot be included in one totality with man. Relations with God depend on grace, not merit.

We are now in a position to look again at peace. Certainly peace requires justice among men, but Christian peace cannot be reduced to such a definition as "each doing his own thing." Peace so defined can be functionally earned; it is a harmony of functions that can be planned as a product. Such peace has its satisfaction; it is the satisfaction of accomplishment, but such peace cannot give newness to life. For a Christian, only disproportion—actually the absence of proportion—is peace. That is why the peace of God is said to pass understanding. (Phil. 4:7) God's peace comes from his presence, and personal presence, we have seen, surpasses the power of understanding. The intimate presence of the absolute Otherness of God calls us to continual newness and creativity; it is completely different in kind from a functional uniformity which can be described and programed. It is the origin of meaningfulness and the spring of life.

Peace, for a Christian, is a gift; the absolute difference of another person, if we are to know it, must give itself to us. That is why it is always a revelation. Wages, however, are understandable; they are something we bargain over. The peace of God passes understanding because it is a gift that surpasses justice, just as the infinitude of a person surpasses every limited personal function. It is that fact, however, that enables God's peace to be the source of justice and the perfection of justice. Anything that can be formalized, like the equality and proportionality of justice—money, social position, power, leisure—is totally different from personal presence, which can only be lived. The infinitude of presence cannot be apprehended from the outside, and neither can true peace, which is an experience of infinitude that can only be given by the presence of one who is Infinite; such an experience, I have tried to show, is the awakening of the infinitude which we are. That experience is nothing less than our *infinition,* to use Levinas' terminology again.

When the Father gives man time in Jesus Christ by making it possible for his future for us to be present with us as a man, the Father gives us a distance from physical defeat and from total passivity in the world. By being with us *first* as a gift of love for which we have no responsibility, the infinite presence of the Father in Christ places us as persons beyond all threatening catastrophes in the world. Without compromising our engagement as persons, peace that we are able to preceive through our senses always involves distance: land- and seascapes are peaceful when we see them from afar, panoramically. That way our wholeness as persons is not attacked, and in our wholeness we grasp the view before us in its wholeness. Integrity matches integrity. Laboratory experiments indicate that animals remain peaceful even in the presence of something that threatens them—if the threatening agent is kept far enough away.

When we are anxious and hard pressed, nervous, and frayed, how frequently it is because we feel that we do not have time to do what is expected of us; our obligations are so immediately upon us that they overwhelm us. Overwhelmed by the presence of our tasks, we are prevented from being our resourceful, creative selves; we feel so bound that we have nowhere to turn. Another way of saying the same thing is that we are so immediately besieged that the present destroys our future. When we are creative, we think from the future into the present. Only because we transcend the present in the dimensionalities of the past and future can we see the present in its proper perspective.

The thing we must remember is that the present of man is always in a perspective; there are always the temporal past and future beyond it which somehow are also us. To be overcome by any one dimension of time is demonic. The personal presence of God changes death for us precisely because its infinitude already places us temporally beyond death with Christ. The presence of the future in the present, which is the Father's gift to man in Christ, separates man as a person from demonic possession by the present—even when death is present. A young child first learns about distance in space. What he wants but does not have is "over there." If he matures in Christ, he learns that it is distance in time that secures his peace; he can never be destroyed in the present, for he already lives in the future with Christ.

Having a distance from what is happening to him in the present, man cannot be threatened by the present. He is at the same time able to be at peace and be creative; in fact, his creativity is the manifestation of his peace. The transcendence that structures the latter is what empowers the former.

Peace, then, is the transcendence of personal presence above and through problems. It can be described a number of ways: as personal integrity in the face of fragmentation; as the primacy of historical fullness over the abstract and incomplete; as the type of distance from the particular that prevents us from being squeezed by parts but requires that we be engaged with the whole.

I have spoken of the sending of the Son by the Father. It was because the Father loved the world with a fully historical, personal love that he sent his Son into the world. Once present as a fact in the world, the presence of the Father's love overflowed the Son and recreated the world through the historical life, death, and defeat of death by Jesus Christ. In his turn, Jesus sent other people into the world in that same love of the Father. The sending of the Seventy is such an instance, and the nature of Christianity is revealed by the action. Sent by love as the Son himself was, what did the Son commission his disciples to bring to the world? "Peace." That was the first thing Christ told those whom he sent out to say to people. "Whatever house you enter, first say, 'Peace be to this house!' "(Luke: 10:5) Peace is *the* Christian salutation because everything Christian begins with it and is found within it. Throughout the centuries of Christianity, as in Judaism before it, "Peace," has been the greeting par excellence. Paul almost always began his letters with the words, "Grace to you and peace from God our Father and the Lord Jesus Christ." Francis of Assisi's first greeting to all men was,

"The Lord give you peace." In his commissioning of the apostles after he had overcome death, as recounted in John's Gosple, Jesus' first words to them were "Peace be with you." After we are told that "the disciples were glad when they saw the Lord," "Jesus said to them again, 'Peace be with you. As the Father has sent me, even so I send you.'" (John 20:-19–21.) Love is a sending—a going—and what it brings is peace.

All men, as Christ himself, are sent into the world to bring peace, but they cannot bring what they do not have. Apart from that, there is a corollary to the fact that men are sent into the world to bring peace; it is that peace is to be found only *in the world.* Christian peace, at any rate, cannot be found outside it, for the mission of Jesus was to bring God's peace into the world. A gift must be received where it is given. The peace offered by Christianity is not a prize people get for escaping the world; it is power for staying in the world. It is "staying power."

The gift of God's presence in our lives which has traditionally been called "grace" is always a call to us from beyond us. But a call is itself a structure; it says one thing rather than another, and is always spoken in a structured situation—i.e., has meaning for particular circumstances—which is only another way of saying that it is always spoken in a world. God's presence to man is a source of strength and assurance to him, but a person must be in a situation before the help appropriate to that situation can be offered to him. One cannot stand on the shore and be helped to swim, nor can a person who denies that he had a problem be helped to solve it. The presence of a mathematician will do no good if a student denies that he is doing mathematics. Peace can only be found in the world, not outside of it, for it is God's gift to the world: to attempt to avoid the world is the one sure way of refusing the gift.

As indicated earlier, the attempt to escape from the world

is an effort to escape from ourselves. If peace is something given to us where we are, we must admit being where we are in order to receive it. That is why peace requires humility. Many people who want God's peace in their lives cannot find it because they insist on searching for it where it is not given. The presence of God we need for peace is offered to us where we are; by refusing to accept ourselves, we are not real enough to accept the real gift we are intended to receive. Peace is God's presence in the world in which we already live. It overcomes the death we are already dying; it is not an impossible hope in a land of make-believe.

God's presence creates us because it locates us; peace is a perfection of our location in the world, not that location's denial. The peace that comes from God's presence depends upon our self-acceptance, but it also helps us accept ourselves and requires that we accept others. It cannot turn us inwardly and selfishly upon ourselves, enabling us to forget others in personal ecstasy as a drug experience can, because God's presence—its source—is always for others. His presence would not be for us if it were not for others. God's presence makes us and everything about us different; in his presence our only peace is to change and to be agents of his change.

Notes

1. *Complete Works of St. Teresa,* trans. and ed. E. Allison Peers. Vol. II (London: Sheed & Ward, 1957), p. 201.
2. *Ibid.,* p. 351.
3. *Ibid.,* p. 208.
4. *Ibid.,* p. 346 f.
5. *Ibid.,* p. 208.
6. Viktor E. Frankl, *Man's Search for Meaning: an Introduction to Logotherapy,* trans. Ilse Lasch (Boston: Beacon Press, 1962), p. 126.
7. *Ibid.,* p. 130 f.

.7.

God's Presence and Man's Future

Every human being, we have seen, is located in the world through his body, but the body provides the structure for a personal presence extending beyond it. We have examined that presence and tried to understand the presence of God through it. I have also tried to describe the experiential difference God's presence makes in our lives, relating that difference to such themes as man's creation, the temporal nature of human life, body-meaning, and peace.

Of all the themes touched upon, none is nowadays more topical than the nature of time and the role of the future in our lives. In the Introduction we noted that many people—and even nations—in the world today are suffering from "future shock." People are subject to such shock when they are overwhelmed by change, when the future in the form of novelty and change descends upon them too quickly. Alvin Toffler has marshaled the evidence for both the existence of such shock and the factors that produce it in a manner that compels attention. In concluding our own exploration, let us look at some of the significant aspects of contemporary life which are either signs or causes of future shock and see how, in the face of them, the Christian religion as we have considered it speaks to our situation. As we have seen, it is only the future that we can fear or about which we can be anxious. Before concluding, I must say still more about the fundamental meaning of time in our lives.

Because man is a body he is a place and needs location. True as that statement is, however, modern nomadic man minimizes in many ways the stability his ancestors found in physical place. The mobility of present-day man has given him a type of release from place: he can travel so extensively and conveniently that he "doesn't know where he is at." Awaking from sleep, he literally may not know where in the world or where in our solar system he is. The title of the comedy about American tourists, *If This Is Tuesday It must Be Belgium*, evokes a not uncommon confusion. Millions of people every year visit other nations for either business or pleasure—or a combination of the two. In an increasing number of countries, led by the United States, millions of persons change their place of residence every year. There are people —many, but not all, in their teens and twenties—whose work and location in one place lasts only long enough for them to make sufficient money to go somewhere else. Various regions of a country, Toffler points out, need no longer be primary sources of diversity. Colleges now find so great a diversity of viewpoint in any given area that they no longer need to use geographical quotas in their admission criteria: they can admit a diversified student body from almost any state or major city in the nation.

It is suggested by Professor John Dyckman that "allegiance to a city or state is even now weaker for many than allegiance to a corporation, a profession, or a voluntary association."[1] Place commitment—that is, to a physical place—appears to be diminishing in the face of other types of reference. Even commitment to such locations as places of employment

seems to be giving way to loyalties less physically defined—
for example, to professional groups and other common-inter-
est organizations. Highly educated and trained people are
beginning to appear in business and industry whose first loy-
alty is to their profession rather than to the company they
happen to be working for at the moment. Less and less do
they see their location as spatially determined.

But as certain types of spatial differentiation decrease,
temporal differentiation increases. Many of the subcults
found in contemporary society are founded on age rather
than geographic identification. The facility with which we
can now communicate with each other and travel around the
world, while overcoming space, has helped accentuate differences of age. To be sure other factors enter into the picture,
but the ease with which people of different ages can now
communicate with people of their own age, and the economic power different age groups have in an affluent society,
enable such groups to develop identities which were out of
the question in earlier and more primitive societies. Peer
groups and peer-group idols develop almost overnight.
Toffler points out that the once-adequate division of people
into children, young persons, and adults is no longer adequate: we now have to use such categories as "pre-teens,"
"sub-teens," "post-teens," and "young-marrieds."

Upperclassmen in colleges frequently find that a communication gap exists between themselves and underclass-
men in their own schools. It is not just the advance in communication and transportation that has brought about this
general situation; a most important additional factor is the
pace of change in the world today. As the speed of change
increases in our environment, the difference between age
groups is magnified.

The aspects of contemporary society we have just been
reviewing illustrate the transience of present-day living. One
of the cultural factors inducing future shock in our day is the

temporariness of life, that is, the increasing turnover we experience in our relationships with things, places, people, and organizations. Exposed to temporariness in all the areas of life mentioned, people are finding it harder and harder to make commitments reaching into the future. They do not want long-term commitments or involvements. "Minimum-involvement housing" is one answer; it is found by living in an all-maintenance-provided apartment instead of buying and maintaining one's own home. Almost anything—clothing, automobiles, household appliances, glasses for a party, nursery equipment, sickroom needs—things people once thought they had to buy, can now be rented. The temporariness of personal contacts encourages people to commit themselves to each other as little as possible, and the stability men once enjoyed in close, long-term friendships seems increasingly threatened.

Transience is not the only feature of contemporary life that can induce future shock, however. Man's increasing exposure to novelty and diversity also contributes to his discomfort. We are confronted not merely with change—the usual change of the seasons, for example—but with *novel* change. And as if novel products alone were not enough, the common satisfaction of basic needs afforded by superindustrial society enables people to seek novel experiences just for their own sake. Bored with the satiety of having our basic needs met, we now have the time, money, and means necessary to seek novel experiences for no other reason than to undergo them. Emporia are already being established where the customers buy not a thing but an experiential transportation achieved through sensory stimulation; Toffler remarks that consumers can now collect experiences as they once collected things.

Diversity, in addition to transience and novelty, is an increasingly important factor in our superindustrial culture. The fact that man is his body and sees the world from different points of view is the ultimate assurance that the human

world must be a pluralistic one, but the cybernated produc-
tion of superindustrialism seems on the way to inundating
him with choices. The productive ability of cybernated society is quite capable of submerging us in choices, for in such
a society the diversity and variation of products costs little or
no more than uniformity. Because of cybernated control, the
thrust of superindustrialism is toward diversification; stand-
ardization of life and of products was a mark of the early
stages of industrialism. Never before, for example, have so
many consumers been able to choose between so many varia-
tions as are now possible when a man goes to buy an automobile. As the advertisements say, he can, indeed, "customize"
his car by selecting the features he wants from hundreds of
options made available to him.

But this diversity of contemporary life is not limited to
consumers' choices of manufactured products; it extends
throughout all the dimensions of a person's life-style. Values
which were once commonly accepted by society are now
subject to attack from many different points of view, and
some people claim that values themselves are turning over
faster than ever before. Great numbers and varieties of subcults are arising, frequently competing with each other for
recruits from society at large. Lacking a location in and orientation to the world in which they are secure, people are now
able to try and to discard many different life-styles in a short
period of time. That very fact may work against their ever
finding a style in which they can feel ultimately secure;
knowing they can always switch to something else and feeling that something different will always be available to them,
they may so restrain their commitment to what they are
doing at the moment that they never know it for what it truly
is.

Overcome by the surfeit of choices, a person may be so
disoriented in his decision-making abilities that he retreats
from reality, turning to the use of drugs or to an irrational

mysticism for comfort. Alternative but equally inadequate responses to high-speed change in the analysis of Toffler are the outright denial of change, limited specialization within it, obsessive return to the past, or attempted oversimplification of the actual condition of the world.

None of these responses to rapid change will do: their adoption may psychologically enable certain individuals to endure, but if adopted on a large scale they will only increase the problems of mankind. Even the individual, if he wants to survive as a full member of the world in which he lives, "must become infinitely more adaptable and capable than ever before. He must search out totally new ways to anchor himself, for all the old roots—religion, nation, community, family, or profession—are now shaking under the hurricane impact of the accelerative thrust."[2] As Toffler goes on to state, the problem "is not . . . to suppress change, which cannot be done, but to manage it. If we opt for rapid change in certain sectors of life, we can consciously attempt to build stability zones elsewhere. . . . To design workable stability zones, however, to alter the larger patterns of life, we need. . . . first of all, a radically new orientation toward the future."[3]

We must recognize two truths about a person's relationship to change: (1) there is a limit to the amount of change anyone can tolerate; and (2) only secure people can welcome change and use it as a vehicle for growth—insecurity forces one to fight change, resist it, or deny it. Since only secure people can welcome change and control it, the need is now felt for new ways to anchor ourselves in time; because there is a limit to our tolerance for change, we must seek "a radically new orientation toward the future."

Many people would agree that the roots men once had in reality are now being laid bare and shaken by the force of rapid change. The ineffectiveness—indeed, the meaninglessness—of many time-honored forms of religious expression in today's world offers a convincing illustration of the storm raging around our institutions. But some rooting in reality there must be. I believe that personal relationship with the different God we have been discussing provides the basic rooting and orientation for which so many people are seek-ing, and which all men need.

We have seen the source of meaning in the universe to be God's absolute difference from us and his presence to us. In the presence of God we cannot be threatened by the ulti-mate meaninglessness of life, even though the possible choices we may be asked to make in the world dizzy us by their number. The fact of our creation, experienced as the presence of God, stabilizes our life, but in a way which con-stantly calls us to creative and new dynamic expression. The security of being loved completely (that is, of being loved too much from our selfish point of view, which is the meaning of the Christian doctrine of creation) is the condition of an "identity crisis" Christians welcome as it calls them into the future.

Our exploration of trust and hope has tried to give mean-ing to the role of time in our lives, showing how that role relates us to the presence of God. We have seen how hopeful living, pointing us toward the future, requires a certain kind of past and is impossible without trust in a presence which is present. The historical nature of Christianity's revelation has shown time—and promises which necessarily involve the future—to be the very "stuff" of Christian living. Made co-creators with the Father in his continuing creation of the universe through the Son, Christians are meant to be mold-ers and leaders of change.

The sacraments, and especially the Holy Eucharist, show how time should be used. Consecration, we saw, takes time, and all time is meant to be consecrating. Sacramental living is temporal living toward the future.

Of course, recognizing our orientation toward the future and feeling secure in the face of change are not all there is to solving man's problems in a fast-changing world. Hard problems remain. Specific decisions cannot always be made with certitude on the basis of general attitudes alone. The presence of God is not magic; it does not save one from work and anguish in the world, but it does motivate one to face reality for what it is. It enables us to bear the responsibility which is ours in change, and it motivates us to do the work that hard decisions in the world require. Above all, since redemption and hope in Christ have the structure of the world within them and are offered to men only within the world, due to the *incarnation* of the Word of God, Christian redemption requires that man not flee the world or turn his back upon it.

But there is still more to be said about a person's relation to time. The meaningfulness of time has been a problem for man as long as he has questioned the universe around him and his life within it. Recognizing that what is foreign to a person's experience is meaningless to him, I have been stressing the experiential dimension of Christianity and the presence of God. Our task now is to continue that emphasis in additional considerations of time. Only a search for the experiential meaning of time can help us in our present crisis for, as has been pointed out, it is our *experience* of temporal change that subjects us to future shock. At the experiential level, I suggest, personal presence alone makes time meaningful.

From the beginning of his existence in the world man has had to come to terms with the temporal nature of his life. Death was his questioner. Before philosophers developed explicit theories about the nature of time, man learned to live and deal with it through ritual and religion. Later on, he tried to theorize about time and to explain it conceptually, but his ideas, no matter how fully developed, offered no experiential solution to his problem. Why? Because ideas in themselves are static; they do not change, for they are timeless. The idea "young" never grows old; the idea "hot" never becomes cold. The idea "life" never dies—while, oddly, the idea "time" is not temporal, and the idea "future" is not future.

Ideas lack the movement of time because they are abstracted from the moving lives and thoughts of men; abstracted from time, they are necessarily less than the temporal reality from which they are removed. Ideas themselves are impotent: people can freeze to death while thinking about heat; they can be mizers while thinking about generosity. It is *men* of ideas who get things done, not ideas themselves. Ideas are related to temporal reality by subtraction, as it were; thus they can never fully explain the reality from which they are taken.

Personal presence, on the other hand, can help us understand time, for personal presence is a fullness always overflowing the present. Wanting to express ourselves as persons, we feel an immediate kinship with time, for the expression of our presence—and the expression of the presence of other people to us—requires a constantly new future in which more can be said than we or others have said in the past. Constantly requiring a future going beyond the present, personal presence produces the past; the past consists of previous futures whose expression we have gone beyond. Personal presence explains time by what we are; it fills time and makes time necessary. It is not off to one side of time as ideas are; it does not deny time as ideas do.

Through the ages men have puzzled about the peculiar "extension" of time. The past is neither the present nor the future; the present is neither the future nor the past; the future is neither the past nor the present. Yet in some mysterious way past, present, and future are all dimensions of time. Because the dimensions of time stand outside each other, they have been called the "ecstasies" of time by Martin Heidegger. The question is, what can hold the ecstasies of time together? Our answer is: the inexhaustibility of personal presence within them!

Because the expression of personal presence *requires* a past, present, and future—as earlier indicated—it unites them. The personal presence which uses them gives the past, present, and future a reason for existing together: they are all expressions of *it*.

The rapid change experienced in the world today makes us question the meaning of the future; for many, the future is an increasing cause of anxiety and fear. If our lives and our relation to the future are to be positively meaningful, an ultimate Source is needed which can give constructive meaning to all the possible futures that may threaten us.

Meaning can ultimately originate, we have seen, only because expression is volunteered from an inexhaustible speaker who will not abandon his words. We have also seen that meaning limits—that is to say, destroys—anarchy and arbitrariness. Meaning gives reasons why things are as they are. The moments of time in their numerical sequence are completely relative to each other and therefore have no ultimate significance in themselves; they always relate to each other in the same way no matter what the contents of time happen to be.

The complete relativity of the measurement of time oppresses and destroys us as persons; it is the aspect of time we try to flee. Oh, how I want this moment of fun to last! I waited for it so long—but a glance at the hands of the clock tells me that time is rushing on it spite of my wishes. Another day I am upset, anticipating an operation I do not want to have. If time would only speed up so that all would be over, I think to myself; but the hands on the clock continue their same course at their same speed. The measurement of clock time pays no attention to the meaning of our lives; it is completely relative to itself and to other impersonal movements that equally ignore us.

The location of time in the presence of a God who is Absolute Other gives time as a whole a significant meaning. The presence of God to time and in time gives the moments of time a depth which they do not have in their relativity to each other. Because of God's presence to time as the Source of all meaning, more can be meant at any given time than its numerical course alone could bring to that moment. Such meaning is precisely what entered history in the Incarnation. The meaning of *all* time can be given to *a* time if the Source of time chooses a time in which to be intimately present. Christians believe Jesus Christ to be that presence.

God's presence will not allow the future to be meaningless or harmful. Because there are infinite resources in the presence of God which have yet to be revealed in time, no moment can be so bad that God cannot redeem it by bringing new meaning to it from outside it. The realization of that fact is the anchor of Christians, and is meant to be the anchor of all men, in the face of change: the future is certain in the sense that its ultimate meaning is secure. It will never be meaningless. The meaning of the future is absolutely sure in that it will ultimately glorify God, the Source of all meaning and therefore the only meaning.

The primacy of God as a Person gives the future of man stability, for a person can always bring a word to time which the mere sequence of time cannot bring by itself. Such is the significance brought to time by Jesus Christ, the Word of the Father. Because God is ultimate Person there is always an alternative to any moment of time and every word of man.

In our earlier discussion of time it was said that in Jesus Christ the future dwells in our present, and that fact enables us to live the certainty of the future in the uncertainty of the present. Christ's resurrection from the dead and the fact that the life he now lives is the future we hope for, assures us that the future is ultimately for our benefit, not our destruction. In Christ's resurrection the future becomes a womb of meaning instead of a threat to meaning; the presence of the future in Christ becomes a source of comfort, not despair.

We cannot see the future clearly and explicitly even in Christ, but we do not need to, for we are assured by its presentation to us in Christ's life after death that it is on our side. Specificity—seeing where and what things are—is furnished by the present; general assurance and security, on the other hand, is furnished the Christian by the future.

The future is able to "dwell within our present" because of the presence of God to us; as the source of time's meaning, God's presence guarantees time. To trust *his* presence translates for us into trusting the future (as if it were present).

If men were truly convinced of the presence of God in time and of the fact that time is meant to be the servant of their expression, they would not hesitate to use it for the benefit of persons. A fatalistic and materialistic view of time which gives it power in its own right would be impossible. People would not be afraid to try to be more of a person in time instead of pretending to wait and see where time will lead them. Only men (and God) lead men; to pretend that time of itself can lead us anywhere is simply a way of letting other men lead us by default.

Decisions will still be hard, as I have said, and there is no guarantee that all our decisions will be the right ones, but ultimately we must know, in a way that gives us nerve enough to commit ourselves in decisions, that time is *for* man —not something against him. In Jesus, God captures time for us without destroying time's movement.

Although I have spoken primarily of the role of Jesus Christ in winning the future for us, we should notice that in Scripture, when the presence of the future in the present is spoken of, it is usually in terms of the gift of the Spirit. There is no contradiction here, for as St. Paul said, "the Lord is the Spirit, and where the Spirit of the Lord is, there is freedom." (2 Cor. 3:17) The gift of the Spirit is freedom in the world, for the Spirit, sent to men at Pentecost after the resurrection and glorification of the Son, brings the power of the future to us.

The author of the Epistle to the Hebrews speaks of those "who have tasted the heavenly gift, and become partakers of the Holy Spirit, and have tasted the goodness of the word of God and the powers of the age to come. . . ." (6:4 f.) The Holy Spirit has otherwise been spoken of as the "guarantee," the "first payment" or "pledge," in the present, of the future inheritance the Father has promised mankind in Christ. (Cf. Eph. 1:13 f.) To live in the Spirit of Christ is already to have tasted the future, and so to be free and unbound in the present.

The Spirit *leads* us into all truth; by leading us the Spirit *moves* us. (John 14:17, 26: 1 John 5:7; Rom. 8:14.) In Scripture the presence of the Spirit is constantly compared to the refreshment of cool water. But the refreshment that the Spirit brings is not rest from change; it is refreshment through change. As we noticed earlier, St. Paul describes life in the Spirit as a constant transformation "from glory to glory." (2 Cor. 3:18 AV) In all politeness, and truly, it may be said that people who do not want change should go to hell! Even in this world nothing is harder to put up with than boredom. The routine and never-changing is hell in this life; why should it be any different after death?

Life after death is constant change (that is, growth in the love of God), and if one believes life in this world is preparation for the "next life," the only way he can begin to prepare himself is by beginning to change here.

The essence of Christian presence, and so the essence of Christian ministry, is the concerned presence in the world of an alternative to the world. Such a presence guarantees the world a *future*, a real future, one better than the present no matter what the present is. The guarantee of the future results from the infinitude of God's love for the world; it is the thoroughness of his redemptive love. His love for us is so great that it never ceases to be creative, and we can never cease to be creative in it.

In the presence of God men discover meaning *for* the

world because such meaning is not *of* the world. The world needs ultimate meaning given to it from beyond it, for of itself it is a totality within which everything is relative. But God's presence also keeps the world relative—keeps it, that is, from being turned into an absolute by those who live within it. Thus the primacy of persons is maintained in the world.

Christians are not to sell, force, cajole, threaten, or make bargains with other men in God's name, for they are neither the proper judge nor the source of whatever success their religion may have. Their only ministry is to proclaim, witness to, and through their presence *be* the presence of a creative alternative to the world. They are to hold out a future which is completely—not partially—meaningful for every person who has ever lived!

Christians will always try to express the reality of God's presence in the world in specific and concrete ways, participating in the activities of the world as their bodily incorporation in the world requires. But even if there is nothing they can do, and no alternative within the world they can suggest—even if they are reduced to suffering or outward passivity—the integrity and peace of their presence to others will constantly testify to the absolute difference of God from man, and so to the ultimate meaningfulness of life among persons.

Notes

1. Quoted in Alvin Toffler, *Future Shock* (New York: Bantam Books, 1971), p. 92.

2. *Ibid.*, p. 35.

3. *Ibid.*, p. 379.

Epilogue

In time of need, it is the presence of another person alone that makes life bearable. A simple back-rub or any other stroke of personal concern says everything. But necessary as we may feel personal presence to be at times, most people find it too intense to bear all the time.

Christianity is a religion which claims that because we begin to exist only in the presence of God, that presence, the source of our accountability, is at the same time the source of freedom, creativity, and all meaning.

To experience presence as release and freedom, to experience the intensity of presence as the intensity of peace and love instead of as the interference of an intruder, is to begin a new kind of life.

That life draws man beyond himself and beyond death, enabling him to live the certainty of the future in the uncertainty of the present.

In such a religion, God, man, and life in the world are "different." If any one of the three is not different, Christianity has either been disproved or what has claimed to be Christian has been shown to be non-Christian.

One way or another, what I have tried to say should make a difference.

The difference that should be denied is the one sometimes made which divides Christians. Because of the experience of an increasing number of people today—an experience somewhat reminiscent of the early days of the church—the "gift of tongues" and other claimed manifestations of the Spirit are again being widely discussed in the church. A special "baptism of the Spirit," accompanied by ecstatic feelings and such gifts as that of "tongues," is beginning to be suggested as the true mark of a *real* or *full* Christian. In some parish churches "in" and "out" groups of Christians are being informally, if not formally, drawn along such lines.

The intensity and frankness brought to the religious lives of those who have claimed baptism in the Spirit are matters of public record. Public testimony as well as intimate cells of worshipers are two marks of some of the stirrings mentioned at the beginning of this book. That same intensity and frankness, however, continue to cause other people to analyze the behavior in question exclusively in terms of psychological and sociological factors.

In a psychological and social world all behavior has psychological and social dimensions, so analysis of any behavior, including the religious, in those terms is instructive. The fact of such analysis is not automatically destructive. But in the name of Christian revelation itself, one may say that any attempt to divide Christians into classes on the basis of charismatic gifts is destructive. St. Paul handled the matter well in his own day, and his advice is still good. (Cf. 1 Cor. 12, 13, 14; Rom. 12, 14:19, 15:1–3.)

All Christians are called to new life in the Spirit. We have explored that life to some extent, but it may be well to add a final clarification of it here. Life "in the Spirit" is in no way opposed to, or more than, life "in Jesus Christ." The Spirit does not add any revelation of the Father to the revelation brought by the Son; the Spirit, instead of minimizing the Son, enables human beings to recognize the Son. "Therefore I want you to understand that . . . no one can say 'Jesus is Lord' except by the Holy Spirit." (1 Cor. 12:3)

A unique but central feature of the New Testament revelation is Jesus' reference to God as "my Father." For a human being to claim such intimacy with God was unheard of in Jesus' day, but the shock to his hearers did not end there. The word Jesus used for the Father was the Aramaic baby word, *abba*. Jesus referred to God the Father with a slight refinement of the babble an infant uses when first referring to his human father. The intimate way in which Jesus lived with God was shocking to his contemporaries, but it was that very intimacy he came to share with all men. Praying the prayer we know as *his*, even we have been told to call God *our Father* in Christ's familiar fashion. We have God as our *Abba*.

Can the Spirit do more than that for us? No. We are told that "God has sent the Spirit of his Son into our hearts, crying, 'Abba! Father!' " (Gal. 4:6) St. Paul further states that when we cry "Abba! Father!" it is the Spirit who bears witness that we, as children of God, can be no more than "fellow heirs with Christ." (Rom. 8:15–17) The Spirit is said in the Fourth Gospel to glorify the Son, "for he will take what is mine [the Son's] and declare it to you." (John 16:14)

The Son showed he was Son by immediately relating to the Father, not by making claims about himself as Son. Jesus nowhere claimed to be the Son of God; it was by doing the *Father*'s will that he was recognized by others to be the Father's Son. Similarly, the Spirit shows he is the Spirit of the Son, sent by the Father, by presenting—making present—the Son, not by claiming to be the Spirit. The Spirit makes no claim to a new revelation beyond Christ. The Spirit makes the glorified Son present with us, as indicated earlier; indeed, the full sending of the Spirit, we read, was even held up until Jesus was glorified. The Gospel according to St. John states that "as yet the Spirit had not been given, because Jesus was not yet glorified." (John 7:39)

There should be no confusion about Christian life in the Spirit, Christian spiritualism, or what a Christian spiritualized body is.

Life in the Spirit is now to live the certainty of Christ's glorified body under the conditions of the present world! That is what it means to be a spiritual body. By the Spirit, Christians become *filled* bodies; they are filled with the fullness of God, his meaning—which is to say, the meaning of Christ. To live *with* Christ, instead of thinking *about* him, is the fullness of the Spirit.

Being incapable of empty lives, for "in him [Christ] the whole fullness of deity dwells bodily," Christians Spiritualize the world by bodily extending Christ's meaning throughout it. In that way both men and the world become filled with God. Such fullness is the purpose of creation.

73 74 75 76 77 10 9 8 7 6 5 4 3 2 1